TALL

Love and Journalism
in a Six-foot World

Nancy Stancill

To Dan & Mary Beth,
Enjoy!
Love, Nancy

Black Rose Writing | Texas

First printing

The author has tried to recreate events, locales and conversations from his/her memories. In order to maintain anonymity in some instances, the author may have changed the names of individuals and places. The author may have changed some identifying characteristics and details such as physical properties, occupations and places of residence.

ISBN: 978-1-68433-590-9
PUBLISHED BY BLACK ROSE WRITING
www.blackrosewriting.com

Printed in the United States of America
Suggested Retail Price (SRP) $15.95

Tall is printed in Georgia

*As a planet-friendly publisher, Black Rose Writing does its best to eliminate unnecessary waste to reduce paper usage and energy costs, while never compromising the reading experience. As a result, the final word count vs. page count may not meet common expectations.

Dedicated in loving memory of my mother and father,
Phyllis Harrill Stancill Pruden and Godfrey Wells Stancill.

"A hearty salute to Stancill for her frank narrative of walking tall in the world. Walk on, I say, walk on!"

—Donald Morrill, author of *Beaut*

"A coming-of-age story typically ends when adolescence stops, but no one ever stops being their height, so when does the coming-of-height story end? In Nancy Stancill's *Tall,* the personal journey of a taller woman culminates beyond acceptance—when the unchangeable recedes in importance. "I felt valued and useful. My tallness didn't matter; my competence to do the job did." This is the real tall girl triumph. Indeed, it's an every girl triumph.

As someone who achieved my full adult height of 5-foot-7 at age 12, I related to Stancill's adolescent fear of drawing unwanted attention, and I was drawn in reading Stancill's lifelong reflection on the challenges and advantages of her tallness. Hurray for Stancill and her "glory in my height."

—Catherine Moore, author of
Borrowings of the Shan Van Vocht

ACKNOWLEDGMENTS

How does one thank everyone who participated in the making of a life? Probably I owe thanks to hundreds of people. Since I'm unable to mention everyone who has touched my life, I'm reserving my appreciation to friends and journalists who helped me with this book.

Major thanks to Dannye Romine Powell and Steve Johnston, whose suggestions and thoughtful editing were crucial. Maureen Ryan Griffin, writing teacher extraordinaire, kept me on track. Her students offered valuable feedback.

Thanks to friends who read and critiqued the book: Pam Kelley, Julia Edmunds, Karen Garloch and Judy Tell.

Thanks to many former *Charlotte Observer* editors who helped me develop as a writer and editor:

Steve Gunn, Jim Walser, Mary Newsom, Cindy Montgomery and Mike Weinstein.

Thanks to Don Mason, retired *Houston Chronicle* editor, who handled with great skill my American Educational Complex stories and all other investigative stories I did at the Chronicle.

Major appreciation goes to my husband, Len Norman; son Jeffrey Norman and his wife, Beth Norman, and siblings Diane Hall, Melinda Poe, Steve Stancill, Jane Stancill and their spouses.

TALL

CHAPTER 1
CUTTING INGRID'S LEGS

As a teenager, I was beginning to enjoy reading the Sunday newspaper, especially the widely popular *Parade* magazine.

I would sit in my favorite chair in our den and page through *The Roanoke (Virginia) Times*, looking for the colorful supplement.

On that Sunday, the magazine's cover, "How to Shorten Too-Tall Girls," made me catch my breath.

I was 15, living in the small town of Radford in southwest Virginia and hating my life as a shy, 6-foot-tall high school sophomore. I was old enough to have survived the ubiquitous bullying that shadowed my existence as a gangly child turned awkward teenager. But I still towered over most of my class – male and female – was painfully introverted and had no expectations for a dating life any time in the foreseeable future.

I devoured the lengthy story of Ingrid Westman, "a tall, slim, beautiful Swedish nurse of 21, happy and content because she is popular with men," author Lloyd Shearer wrote.

Five years earlier, according to the story, Ingrid was "perennially miserable" because she was 6-foot-$1\frac{1}{2}$ and "felt like a big bear...I felt isolated, alienated like a freak in a circus."

She and her parents sought a medical solution from the chief surgeon at the now-defunct Institute for the Crippled in Sweden. Eventually, they persuaded the doctor to perform osteotomies on both legs. In two operations, the surgeon removed $2\frac{3}{8}$ inches from the shaft of her thigh bones and reattached them with plates and screws.

Just a few months later, the article said, "Ingrid was back on her feet, much happier for her shorter stature."

As I read the story, I thought about whether I should try to get such an operation. Maybe that was the answer to my despair over my tallness. Should I mention it to my parents? Since it involved a Swedish woman in a faraway foreign country, I never did. I knew they would never consider anything so radical.

But that story haunted me over the years. As I thought about growing up tall in America, I wanted to read it again. *Parade* magazine in 1964 was carried in the Sunday edition of most major papers, so the story had resonance. I finally got a copy.

Ingrid Westman was pictured as I'd remembered her: Same bright smile, bouffant hairdo and the professional look of a prim pinafore and pillbox cap nurses wore in the 1960s. The article hadn't aged well. It was patronizing and dripped with unintended sexism. The male writer assumed that the woman had no interests or life goals other than dating and eventually marrying "the right man."

My reaction this time was starkly different. Instead of being mesmerized with the tantalizing possibility of losing a few inches, as I was as a troubled teenager, I was horrified at what this attractive woman had done.

Westman and her parents had begged for a risky, untested operation to cut into her leg, remove some thigh bone and tinker it back together with metal and screws, a procedure that could have caused infection. It could have maimed her for life. Two months later, she did it again with the other leg and endured a recovery period of two more months. She could have ended up with legs that didn't match, an uneven gait. Luckily, that didn't happen.

All it did was reduce her height by a measly $2\frac{3}{8}$ inches – a result that seemed hardly worth the risk.

The writer quoted several other doctors who disagreed with attempting such an operation, saying Westman eventually would have adjusted to her height. Her physician, in his defense, said he'd made her wait a year to make sure before he performed the surgery.

I could definitely relate to Westman's feelings. I've never been allowed to forget that I'm six feet tall. Strangers who wouldn't dare ask how much you weigh feel free to bombard you with intrusive questions or inane comments about your height.

I was unable to locate Westman to find out how the Swedish woman's life unfolded after her radical surgery. I hope that her ecstatic reaction to shedding a couple of inches lasted and contributed to her life satisfaction. I'm glad such a controversial operation didn't become a worldwide trend.

More common than Ingrid's surgery, primarily in Europe and Australia, was administering hormones before a potentially tall woman reached puberty to essentially stunt her growth.

No one knows how often U.S. physicians, pressured by worried parents, ordered hormones for girls, but their use appears rare. A doctor with a national endocrine association said the medical regimen essentially ended fifty years ago, as more physicians became aware of the dangers of giving hormones to preteen girls.

Giving hormones to short boys to heighten their growth has been much more common in this country.

Scattered research indicates that hormone therapy was prescribed to females in a few other countries, most often from the 1950s to the early 1990s. Many girls who submitted to attempts to reduce their adult height through years of taking hormones suffered fertility and other reproductive problems later in life. The hormone treatments basically ended once the problems received publicity.

Interviews with a researcher in Tasmania, Australia, indicated that a couple of dozen tall girls in that area were treated with hormones by the same doctor in the early 1990s. Most of the women said they regretted the hormone therapy because it was foisted upon them without their consent and left them with enduring problems without significantly reducing their height.

I didn't know about hormone therapy for girls until I began researching this book. In the small cities where we lived, I'm guessing my parents never heard of it. That turned out to be a very good thing.

CHAPTER 2
KINDERGARTEN BRINGS A REVELATION

I was in a Methodist Church kindergarten in Elizabethton, Tenn. when I first realized I was tall for my age. Like the rest of my classmates, I'd brought a small rug from home to use for naps. But my legs were too long for the striped rectangular rug, so my feet stretched over to the bare floor. They felt exposed, cold and uncomfortable. Most of my classmates were shorter and rounder and fit snugly on their rugs. Naptime, which came after lunch, wasn't very restful for me. I didn't tell my teachers or complain to my parents. I just knew that I was taller – and different than most of my young classmates.

I was the skinny second child of Godfrey and Phyllis Stancill. My parents weren't unusually tall adults. My dad was barely 6-foot-1, just an inch taller than I would be. My mother said she was 5-foot-4 in her early thirties. In her nineties with a bad case of osteoporosis, her height dwindled to an even five feet.

My parents' love story started with a chance encounter at the Y Court, a familiar landmark where students at University of North Carolina-Chapel Hill liked to gather.

Phyllis Harrill was a striking junior transfer at UNC in the winter of 1944. My mother was aware that the odds for women students looking for men and marriage were exceedingly good. It was wartime and lots of male students were being called up for military duty. There was a frenetic atmosphere of now-or-never on the campus and in the frenzied relationships between young men and women.

Phyllis sashayed up to a group of handsome male students and started flirting with them. The brunette with the long, dark hair and cute curvy figure was undeniably attractive. Confident and outgoing, she caught the eye of a handsome, dark-haired farm boy from Washington, North Carolina. Soon they were dating seriously. The small-town Tennessee girl had met the fellow she'd marry. Their life together would produce five children and result in a 50-year union that lasted until my father's death in 1995.

Two of the children were destined to be tall. My brother Steve is nearly 6-foot-6, six inches above my height. The other three are moderately tall.

Surely, Phyllis was at the peak of her beauty when she started dating Godfrey. There were certain steps in the hot-and-heavy courtship that I've heard about all my life. He gave Phyllis his fraternity pin within months of their first date and asked her to marry him at UNC's storied Old Well soon after that.

They married in February, 1945 in my mother's hometown of Elizabethton. Their wedding had to be moved up a week because my father had gotten Navy orders to report to San Francisco, and later to Seattle, before he shipped out.

He and my mother had a romantic cross-country honeymoon, stopping on their train journey to visit New Orleans and a few other places they'd never been. But there was sadness and anxiety because they knew they'd be parted by a nasty warfront in the Pacific. Luckily my father returned unscathed.

Four years and one child later, I came into this world in a hurry.

Every year, my mother's birthday call to me included an unsettling description of my birth. She was relaxing with my father and another couple in my parents' back yard at 9 p.m. when she felt the beginnings of labor. My father hurried across the street to borrow my grandparents' car. They drove seven miles to their hospital in Johnson City, traveling at breakneck speed around the curves of the narrow road. They made it to the hospital, but my arrival wouldn't wait for my mother's doctor to arrive or an available delivery room. I was born around 10 p.m. on a stretcher in the hall with a stray nurse attending my mother.

"You couldn't wait to get into this big old world," my mother often said. It's clear that she relished the chance to relive the drama of my arrival.

I was born healthy and a perfectly average seven-pounder. There was no indication that I'd grow up to be tall.

As a young child in the early 1950s, I lived with my parents, older sister Diane and baby Melinda in our modest house across the street from the grander, two-story stucco home of my grandparents.

My mother had grown up in her parents' house. Their home was one of the largest in a quiet residential area with mostly older homes. West 'E' Street had a few old-fashioned two-stories, newer ranch-type houses and a brick church on the short block.

My grandparents, great-grandmother and great-great grandmother (who had raised my grandfather) lived in the big, Moorish-style house on an elevated lot across the street. They provided a lot of things I relished in my early childhood – comfort, security and unconditional love. They were all of average height, none tall.

My grandparents, Roy and Carral Harrill, had moved to Elizabethton from Western North Carolina to follow my grandfather's booming career in insurance and real estate. They brought Mama Long, my beloved great-grandmother, and Granny, my great-great-grandmother, who died when I was three or four. Like many older women of their time, our elderly female relatives had few financial assets, but found refuge and a loving place with my grandparents. In the years before Social Security brought a measure of independence for retirement-age adults, these kind and helpful women found a welcoming home with the younger generation. It was what families routinely did to support their older relatives.

The Great Depression profoundly changed the household's prosperous life. My grandfather's finances soured and like many others, he had to eke out a living for a while.

My great-grandmother lost her meager life savings with the failure of a local bank. My grandmother took the sudden disappearance of the family's investments in stride. The day of the stock market crash, my grandfather came home, sat down with her in the living room and told her he was about to lose a dozen houses he'd acquired during the flush years.

"Sweetie, we're going to lose our property," my grandfather said. "I think I can save one house. Which one do you want?"

My grandmother didn't miss a beat.

"I'll take the biggest one, honey," she said.

That's how my grandparents came to live in the odd but interesting house whose view we could enjoy from our living room picture window. The stucco on the exterior was painted a stark white and the curves at the top of the facade gave it the appearance of a castle. Inside, it was just as idiosyncratic. The stucco walls in the living room were painted in a peach shade, the covered wooden staircase had an oblong window opening into the living room and the same brown wicker upholstered furniture my grandparents used throughout my childhood and later on.

As an adult, when I visited the Thomas Wolfe birthplace in Asheville, I was struck at how much the interior of the author's childhood home reminded me of the inside of my grandparents' house, especially the kitchen and its furnishings. My grandparents' kitchen was small and in need of modernizing, but I don't think it occurred to that thrifty couple to change it. The kitchen had a table with four chairs, worn black linoleum and a small cabinet with a rollout top to make biscuits.

And there were plenty of biscuits for me. I'd go to Mama's (the affectionate nickname we gave my great-grandmother) each afternoon and she'd feed me a snack of cold biscuits with Karo syrup. When I see that familiar brand at grocery stores, I think of Mama, Granny, Pappy and Mommie, (our name for our grandmother) and how they shaped my early life.

My favorite person in the big house across the street was Mama. She was the mother of my grandmother and very protective of Mommie during what appeared to be her occasional bouts with anxiety. Mama had lost her own mother as a teenager and helped raise nine younger siblings. Tragedy struck again when her husband died early in their marriage from an injury. She started a boarding house to earn a living, cooking and taking care of millworkers and schoolteachers. She sent her children to college, only to lose her other daughter in 1918 in the massive flu epidemic.

Despite a life of travails, Mama was the most positive person I've ever known and she paid a lot of attention to me. She taught me my alphabet and how to read when I was four. She used copies of *The Upper Room*, a religious magazine, to teach me those basic skills. The other thing we did most days was to sit at the kitchen table and watch the birds splashing in the birdbath in the back yard. She'd laugh with delight and tell me about each type of bird. She loved winter because the snow and cold weather heralded a quieter season. I still share her love of winter, though cold weather is fast disappearing in the Carolinas, where I now live.

This multi-generational household of strong, interesting women made a huge difference in my young life. Across the street, the small, shingled ranch-style house where I lived with my parents had a different atmosphere. They liked to go out with friends, and to buy things for the house, but money was tight, leading to occasional arguments.

CHAPTER 3
HAPPY GIRLHOOD BECOMES BULLYING NIGHTMARE

When I was eight, my family's life was upended by a move from Elizabethton to Radford, Virginia. These two small cities were a mere 125 miles apart and very similar in core values and culture. But to my homesick mother, moving was a catastrophe of unimaginable proportions. To the rest of us, who had never lived anywhere else, it felt decidedly strange.

The reason for the move was simple. My father was working for a chain of small newspapers and he'd been promoted from managing a weekly publication to running a 3,000-circulation daily. With the family now consisting of six with my brother's birth, my father's slim salary couldn't be stretched any farther. Becoming editor and publisher of the *Radford News Journal* was a significant advancement that carried more money and prestige. In the mid-1950s, it was unthinkable that my mother should leave her young children to work.

And while my father was excited about the new challenge, my mother felt bereft at the thought of leaving her extended family across the street. To a young woman who liked regular outings with longtime Elizabethton friends, losing her lifeline of babysitters, meals, and ready advice was painful. I also missed my supportive grandmother and great-grandmother terribly.

But I found Radford more to my liking. I entered the third grade as shy and timorous, but soon made friends at the newly built school and in the neighborhood that sheltered children of all ages.

I look back on my years between eight and eleven as idyllic. I felt physically strong and independent. My summertime days were spent on my beloved pink and white bike. My boundaries, dictated by my parents, included six blocks from the street where we lived.

Halfway along my permitted route was a street corner shaded by a large maple tree where friends often gathered to rest and talk. I loved stopping there if people I knew were hanging out. The other diversion was a small, shabby neighborhood store that had penny and nickel candy. I usually only had a few cents to spend on Mary Jane candies or bubble gum, but the kind husband-and-wife owners didn't seem to mind.

I've talked to many tall women who recall good times at the midpoint of childhood. They didn't worry about how they looked, how they dressed, or whether boys (or the larger society) approved of them.

Then puberty kicked in and their lives would change abruptly. The next few years would shatter my self-image.

Everyone suffers during the awkward years of puberty. But I suspect that during the decades of the 1950s and 1960s, tall girls like me were among the most tormented adolescents. I felt strongly that the preference of boys and society at large was for short, curvaceous and outgoing girls, not tall, skinny and shy females like me. This view is validated by past and present research, which shows that overall, U.S. men prefer women they date and marry to be three inches shorter than their height. Men also believe that shorter women are more nurturing and likely to be better mothers. Taller women are seen to be more assertive and independent.

Though it sometimes seems that U.S. women are getting taller, the average overall height is still 5-foot-4 and hasn't budged in decades. Meanwhile, women from the Scandinavian nations and Netherlands keep getting taller. The average at 5-foot-7 is still climbing.

One theory is that women in those countries have easier lives, with universal kindergarten and other social welfare benefits that translate into happier, taller women and children.

I don't think my six-foot height had anything to do with U.S. societal practices. My parents didn't have any special benefits that might have made their lives easier or their children taller. If anything, their life was harder when I was young because my father had a hard time supporting us all on a newspaper salary. My height seemed to come mainly from heredity.

I grew up (literally) during a time when U.S. pediatricians didn't normally forecast height. My mother says she never realized I was going to be unusually tall until I started shooting up at age 12. By the time I was 14, I'd reached my full adult height of 5-foot-11 3/4. Okay, I was six feet, but I wouldn't admit to that last quarter inch.

I was fearful of drawing attention to my tallness, so as much as possible, I avoided being measured. But between the ages of twelve and fourteen, I gained at least ten to twelve inches of height. I'm estimating, because I know that my son Jeff grew ten inches during the same time period of his life. The difference? He was a male and most people think it's excellent for youths and men to be tall. He topped out at nearly 6-foot-3 and was much sought after by high school girls. I was glad his experience with height was positive, so unlike mine.

Around age 12, during the sixth and seventh grades, I started dreading recess because boys would follow me or taunt me in passing with unwanted nicknames. Their favorites: "Stickweed" and "Toothpick."

I can still hear them saying it as I played kickball or hung out with the girls on the playground. I felt so exposed and unattractive.

Most children get bullied at some point in their school careers, but I wasn't as good as some pre-teens at sloughing it off. I remember crying to my parents about it and they tried to take away the sting by making light of it. My father, my idol and icon, would say when I was about to go to bed, "Time for the toothpick to go into the toothpick box!" He tried to ease the heartache with humor, but it didn't take away the hurt.

I suspect that my mother talked to at least one of my teachers about the bullying, but of course, that hardly ever alters the bad behavior of pre-teen boys. It just makes them sneakier.

I spent a lot of time during those years wondering what cosmic joke nature was playing on me. My parents weren't unusually tall, so why me?

My dad's family included two spinster aunts and a bachelor uncle, all tall and rangy. It was not lost on me that they were unmarried. I'd be like them, I thought gloomily, living alone or with an unfortunate taller sister or brother who'd never find a mate. Aunt Margie, Aunt Miriam and Uncle Henry never seemed unhappy, though. They lived comfortably in their two-story frame house dating from the 1900s on the winding acreage of the family tobacco farm near Washington, N.C.

My paternal grandparents' house was located on the same road, with only a sizable tobacco field between their dwellings. I never heard my aunts and uncle address their single state, but family lore had it that World War I had killed off their presumptive mates, at least those of the women.

I loved my grandparents and other relatives in Little Washington, as it's fondly known, and greatly enjoyed my visits to the farm doing fun things like collecting eggs from the hens. But we only saw my father's side of the family once or twice a year, so I never got to know them as well as my maternal grandparents.

Those years that followed late childhood were disconcerting for me. When was it that I metamorphosed from being a happy little girl to an anxiety-ridden young teen? My tenth birthday, an outdoor cookout for close to a dozen girlfriends, was fun. I enjoyed the outdoor party and don't remember feeling any social anxiety as I devoured the attention – and four hamburgers and hotdogs. I had a hearty appetite at that time of my life but was bone thin.

My father was flourishing as the newspaper's editor and publisher and my parents' worries about money were mostly simmering below the surface. They joined a square dance club, bridge groups and a close-knit Methodist church. My mother was too busy with four children, especially the younger ones, to worry much about me.

During my seventh-grade year, it seemed that my body turned into something unrecognizable. I went from being confident and reasonably athletic to feeling clumsy and oafish as I inexorably added inch after inch. Since Radford had such a small school system, there was no junior high to cushion the changes.

Seventh was the last grade at my sheltered elementary school. The penultimate event was the seventh-grade trip to Richmond, Williamsburg and Jamestown to see the Civil War and Revolutionary War museums and landmarks. The four-day trip was agony for me because boys and girls began pairing off on the bus. My shorter girlfriends had no trouble with this, but I felt like I stuck out like a mighty oak in a forest of saplings. A kind, shorter boy named Eddie eventually sat with me for part of the trip, but with my customary shyness, I couldn't think of much to say to him. I was so relieved when that trip ended.

Radford was too small to have junior high schools or middle schools. So high school was grades eight through twelve. The thought of going to high school was scary. Some of my girlfriends from elementary school were already finding girls they liked better than me. Settling into adolescence exacerbated the "mean girl" syndrome and I was low on the popularity pole. It was a lonely period in my life.

CHAPTER 4
A BABY SISTER

Just before I turned fourteen, my father called his three girls (I think my brother Steve was too young) into the family room one night. I worried about what might come next: a dire announcement of family sickness, divorce or bankruptcy?

He waited until we were all seated to lob an even bigger surprise.

"Your mother's going to have a baby," he said.

My mother, with a sly look, corrected him.

"We're going to have a baby."

"How nice," I said gamely.

In fact, I was flabbergasted and appalled. How dare my parents have sex at their advanced age? How embarrassing.

In reality, they weren't that old. My father was 37 and my mother 39. But I thought our family, with four children, was already bursting at the seams. Most of my friends had only one brother or sister. I had assumed that my sweet, cute baby brother, seven years younger than me, would be the end of the line.

We were all at least three or four years apart, with 17 years that would separate my sister Diane and the upcoming arrival. People freely gawked at us in restaurants as if to imply that our parents were dimwitted or crazy.

I'd wondered what was amiss with my mother. Lately she'd spent a lot of time stretched out on the couch. She generally had a lot of energy during the day, so her lethargy had puzzled and concerned me. She also wore the same Loden green, wrap-around corduroy skirt most days, which also didn't seem like my fashion-plate mother. After the announcement, I understood. She was suffering with the morning sickness of early pregnancy.

I'd reached my maximum height by then and I'd thought glumly that I'd be the tallest of the children. I was excited to think that perhaps the new arrival might eventually carry that banner. We could swap clothes and stories of tall life.

I had to admit that my mother looked great during the latter part of her pregnancy. First Lady Jackie Kennedy was also pregnant and wearing stylish, shorter shift dresses instead of the dowdy two-piece outfits with clownish collars that characterized maternity clothes in the early 1960s. I remember in particular a pink linen shift that looked a lot like what Jackie was wearing.

(When I was about eight, my mother lent her maternity clothes to my aunt. I thought they were talking about fraternity clothes, which left me confused. Perhaps the outfits were for parties?)

Still, despite the growing evidence, I never talked about my mother's pregnancy with friends unless they asked about it. I'd shamefacedly admit it and move on quickly to other topics.

My parents sent me to a five-week camp that summer, so I wasn't in town when the blessed event took place. I was too busy learning to sail, canoe, ride horses and shoot rifles. My mother wanted all of us to experience this particular fancy camp at least once and I was about to reach the camp's maximum age. Two friends from Radford also attended, but as is often the case with three cabin mates, I felt like the one who was usually left out.

I tried not to dwell on what was going on at home until my father called me one afternoon midway through the session.

"You have a new baby sister," he said during the brief long-distance call. (Long-distance was expensive and rare in our family.) "We're going to name her Jane."

"That's really great," I said, but didn't mean it at all.

By a lucky coincidence, my sister Diane was working a shift as a nurse's aide in Radford Hospital that day. Mother's obstetrician called her down to the maternity and delivery floor. She was directed to the delivery room where Jane had just been born. Nurses were finishing weighing, cleaning up and dressing the baby.

They swaddled her in a blanket and handed her to Diane. She carried the newborn out of the delivery suite to our mother's room and introduced her to Daddy.

When I returned from camp a week or so later, my mother was still in the hospital with a painful kidney infection. I visited her in the maternity ward. She was lying in bed when we walked in. She seemed despondent and I couldn't detect much joy over the new arrival.

"I'll never get well," she wailed.

I was slightly alarmed, but knew she sometimes exaggerated.

"Of course, you will," I said.

I stopped at the nursery and met the new arrival, who was bald and to my eyes, a very ordinary looking infant. I couldn't relate to all of the oohing and cooing.

A few days later, my mother returned home with Jane and a baby nurse named Laconia. Previously, during the births of Melinda and Steve, my grandmother and great-grandmother had helped soak up the extra work of a new baby and small siblings.

But we were living three hours away by car, a journey that was almost unthinkable to those two older ladies who never left their small town of Elizabethton.

Laconia, a large, rather stern African American woman, took over with aplomb, sometimes cooking but mostly taking care of Jane. She'd been doing this kind of work for at least twenty years and brooked no interference.

"This is No-No's baby," she told the siblings before shutting the door firmly. No-No was the nickname she preferred.

"She won't let us even see Jane," Diane complained.

Frankly, I didn't like the disruption of a squalling baby. I was used to a certain amount of quiet to read and daydream.

After six weeks, Laconia finished the baby-tending gig. By then, we'd softened toward the kind woman. She was bossy and possessive of Jane, but she made the best hamburgers and fries we'd ever tasted.

Diane and I resumed our customary roles. After our younger siblings were born, we became the self-designated helpers. Diane would watch the children, and I'd cook dinners and late-night desserts. If anyone came over, we'd rush around the rooms and straighten up. I'm not sure why we did this: probably my mother was too busy.

When Jane was five months old, I was babysitting one afternoon while everyone else was out. We were in my father's small study, which had a lumpy sofa. I changed her diaper, took it to the nearby bathroom and heard an ominous bumping sound. She'd rolled off the couch and was screaming. I picked her up and she stopped crying quickly. I decided I wouldn't tell anyone because I'd be in big trouble. I never did mention it until she was grown.

Despite my initial distaste, Jane was so adorable that she melted hearts, mine included. We delightedly repeated her baby words and phrases and imitated her toddler tricks. I was old enough to get some hands-on training with a young child. When I went off to college four years later, it was Jane I'd miss most of all.

When we grew up, we both became journalists. After I moved to North Carolina, I worked for the *Charlotte Observer* and she appropriately worked for its sister paper: the *News & Observer* of Raleigh. Sometimes people would confuse us; we both kept our maiden names and sounded so alike on phone interviews. Neither of us is a reporter anymore but we still love talking about journalism.

The 14-year difference in our ages has disappeared with common experiences. Despite my longings for a tall sister, she turned out to be the runt of the litter: only 5-foot-5. I love her anyway.

CHAPTER 5
NO ROOM AT THE HOUSE

I've always loved Virginia Woolf's "A Room of One's Own," the famous essay in which she says a woman must have money and a room of her own to write fiction.

Her persuasive work always resonated with me in the most basic sense. The title reminded me that I always yearned for a room of my own growing up. I also wanted to write fiction, but it would take many years for that ambition to become reality. As for Woolf's mention of money, I'm afraid that one was a lost cause.

Back to the room of my own, a few facts. During my childhood years, I always shared a room with my older sister Diane. To say that we were simpatico would be an understatement. She used to make me cry by saying that she was adopted and wasn't my real sister. Though I was 3 1/2 years younger, I read her library books and followed her around like a stray kitten. I was happy to share a room with her during those early years.

Besides, if I'd wanted a room of my own then, there wasn't any practical way I'd get it. From my birth to the time I was 11, the six of us lived in three-bedroom, one-bath ranch-style houses. My parents had one bedroom, my younger sister Melinda (and later, my little brother Steve) would have another and Diane and I would share the third.

When we moved to Radford, my dad got a decent promotion and for the first time, my parents were able to build their own larger house. With much excitement, they bought a bare lot and consulted a long list of floor plans. The brick colonial that emerged as the winner had a living room, dining room, tiny den, eat-in kitchen, powder room and family room with a triangular fireplace. Upstairs, there were four bedrooms and two baths. For the first time, our big family had room to spread out.

I remember going to a variety of showrooms to help select carpet, shelves and bathroom fixtures. Consistent with the styles of that time, they chose green, pink and gold bathroom fixtures, busy-looking wallpaper and a different color of paint for each room.

Finally, I thought, there was a chance for me to have a room of my own. I would sit at my small desk like Jane Austen and compose deathless prose. I'd have a large closet and fill it with stylish clothes that complemented my tall stature and thin figure. I'd have a bookshelf and fill it with my favorite books.

Once again, my hopes were dashed. I was ordered to share a bedroom with my four-years younger sister Melinda, who was very sweet, but like most little girls, messy. The room was pink, with pink bedspreads and white curtains with pink trim. Going into adolescence, I hated pink and disliked the clutter generated by the toys of a younger sister. The most fun we had together was decorating the room for Christmas, complete with an artificial, tabletop tree.

I felt cheated when I saw what my sister Diane was getting – cool blue walls, nice antique furniture and a double bed with a pale blue bedspread. But I had hope. In a few years, she'd go to college and I'd inherit her room.

Or so I thought. It was not to be. The fall she began college, my mother decreed that no one could move into Diane's room because she'd come home often and would need to stay in her own familiar room. However, I could go in there and read occasionally.

This seemed manifestly unfair to me. How could I be creative like Virginia Woolf without a room of my own? I just knew I could write if given sufficient solitude. The room, however, was preserved as a shrine to Diane's high school career, complete with faded corsages, cheerleading paraphernalia and numerous pictures of her dressed for dances.

What could I do but capitulate? My mother ruled the house and her decisions were ironclad. Because there was no desk and no hope of a quiet, well-ordered place, I gave up the idea of writing there. Instead, I'd sneak in there and read my parents' potboiler novels with love scenes that offered glimpses of sex to a curious teenager. But my mother always admonished me not to touch or rearrange anything for Diane's increasingly infrequent weekends.

When I complained about not having a room of my own, my family made fun of me, saying I was hardly deprived and should get over it.

Easy for them to say, I thought.

Nobody in my family understood the need of a too-tall, self-conscious teenager for privacy, solitude and a decent place to write, or at least daydream about it. My mother always sighed and said she did the best she could.

No wonder it took me another forty years to write my first novel.

CHAPTER 6
THE TALLEST GIRL AT MY HIGH SCHOOL

I study the girl in the photograph of a high school pep rally. She's decent-looking, with medium-length brown hair, a slender frame and even features. She's wearing a pleated skirt and a pastel sweater. She's half a head taller, or in some cases, a head taller than the other teenagers in the front row. Unlike them, she's not looking at the cheerleaders. Her expression is slightly bored and she's gazing away, seemingly in her own world.

I'm the girl in the photograph, which was posted on Facebook recently by someone in my high school alumni group. I don't remember the picture or the exact date, but the clothes and hairstyle indicate I was a sophomore. I thought of myself as a giant, towering over everyone at my high school, hovering somewhere along the edge of the popular kids, but too unattractive to fit in.

The photograph, however, shows a person who's taller than her fellow students, but hardly freakish looking. This much seems evident. The girl's not paying attention to the cheerleaders because she doesn't like the rah-rah atmosphere of the pep rally and she likely isn't interested in football. In fact, she's not very interested in high school.

I never had an eating disorder, but I'm reminded of deluded young women who stare into the mirror and see themselves as hopelessly overweight though they're as skinny as reeds. I just couldn't see anything but ugliness in my tallness.

Add that to my extreme shyness and my first two years of high school in 1962-64 (eighth and ninth grades in our small town) were miserable.

The forbidding high school building was a traditional two-story edifice perched on a hill at the entrance to the city. Its location indicated its importance to Radford. It was the only high school, housing a small population of 600 students in five grades.

Later, when I was safely ensconced in college, the high school would be mostly destroyed by fire. It was like burning the bridges of my past, which seemed appropriate. Years later, my husband would find an old postcard of the original high school in an antique store. We bought it, not for me, but for Diane, whose memories of the place were considerably happier.

As a fearful eighth grader, I entered the high school with a sense of doom.

In those days, students carried heavy loads of books and notebooks, not backpacks. The lower grades' lockers were located in the basement, so I was always on the edge, or sometimes even late, for my next class. I was stressed out because I was always running behind.

About half the eighth graders were still munchkin-sized and easy to overlook. They weren't happy about that, but I wanted to be like them. Being invisible sounded great to me, certainly preferable to the stares my height elicited. Students in the upper classes basically ignored the eighth and ninth graders unless the younger pupils did something stupid to be mocked. It made for a compelling case for middle school or at least, junior high, where the students were usually more compatible.

My high school academic performance continued to be decent, except for any kind of math or physical education. Math scared me and my body felt too awkward to excel at anything physical. I had skinny weak arms, which made it hard to do pushups or play games of strength like tennis.

Basically, I didn't care enough to strive for straight A's like so many of today's stressed-out students. I could have done a lot better with more effort. However, bringing home a combination of A's and B's seemed perfectly sufficient in those days.

My favorite subject was Latin because it seemed so exotic. I imagined myself clothed in a beautiful flowing white dress with a gold belt, softly strumming on a harp before a class full of entranced male students. Strangely this never happened.

My reality was crushingly different. Some of my female friends had a custom of meeting in the gym before school started and playing basketball. I tried to blend in by joining in the pickup games. Despite my height, I was a terrible player, always out of breath and lacking the sure-footed confidence of other girls. I couldn't shoot a basket if my life were at stake. To this day, I cringe when people ask me if I played basketball in school – the inevitable question put to tall girls.

If there had been a better physical education program for girls in the 1960s, perhaps I would have developed more skills and found a sport that suited me. Track? Volleyball? Rowing? Since physical education was a little of this and a little of that, I never got good at anything. Later, I would envy the girls who benefited by the passage of the federal law known as Title IX in 1972, which prohibits sex discrimination in sports programs. It helped tall girls win scholarships and women's sports to be taken more seriously.

It was as though all of those years of riding my bike had been for naught. My changing body seemed to draw catastrophes – a terrible bike wreck that left lifelong leg scars and a particularly bad encounter with the top of a barbed wire fence. In the latter incident, I was with two friends. One afternoon, we were riding our bikes and came upon a barbed wire fence next to a street we wanted to explore.

The fence was tall with barbed wire at the top. My friends climbed over it safely, but I got caught and cut a gash on the side of my left knee. I don't remember the next part, but I know I got close to a dozen stitches. For the longest time, I could see their imprint and I still can see the scar.

I had loved my lean, active childhood frame. Now it felt weak, disjointed, out of balance. I blamed it all on my height.

As usual, I took refuge in reading, checking out four or five books weekly, especially for my dateless weekends.

But by tenth grade, high school was becoming slightly more tolerable. I was still sensitive about my height and thinness (114 pounds on a six-foot girl is pretty skinny) but I felt somewhat more accepted.

I wasn't driving yet but Brenda, my best friend, had a car and we spent many weekend nights looking for boys. (Not that we'd know what to do if we found them.)

Radford was so small it had only two hangouts for teens: The Hob-Nob and the Biff Burger, two humble fast-food places at opposite ends of town. We'd spend evenings driving back and forth between the two eateries, scouting out the new arrivals of both sexes.

Eleventh and twelve grades had more highlights. I became managing editor of the high school paper and enjoyed the work and camaraderie with budding journalists. I joined clubs and the National Honor Society, credentials that made me feel better about myself.

I had a watershed moment over cheerleading. Diane, now off at college, had been a cheerleader and I felt obligated to try out for that apex of high school success. But I didn't think there was even a remote chance I'd get chosen. The photograph that surfaced a few years ago didn't lie. Just as I was bored in pep rallies, I didn't like what cheerleaders did. I couldn't really imagine myself jumping up and down and screaming about football.

I stewed over it for a while, trying to figure out how to tell my parents. I was sure they'd be disappointed in me.

One night, shortly before tryouts began, I waited until they were alone, then approached them in the family room. I adopted a faux-casual tone to go with my anxious words.

"Cheerleading tryouts are coming up, but I don't want to try out," I said. "Is that okay?"

"Honey, you do whatever you want," my dad said. "You don't have to do anything for us."

Whew! I was so relieved. I'd been afraid they'd insist that I follow my sister to the cheerleading squad. My parents came through by that simple act of acceptance and I never forgot it. You can forgive a lot of less-than-perfect parenting if you know your parents really see you.

Radford teenagers always spent time at nearby Claytor Lake during the hot weather. The summer of my junior year, I found a boyfriend. I was barely 17 and Jerry was a 21-year-old lifeguard. He was slightly shorter, with compelling brown eyes and a shock of dark hair. Soon we were seeing each other, mostly at the lake. My parents predictably didn't like the age difference, though they allowed me to date him.

We went out some that summer, but it obviously meant more to me than to him. He went back to college and by the time snow fell, we'd broken up. I had to give up his class ring, which I'd filled with candle wax and proudly wore on my engagement ring finger. I was back to my mostly dateless state, though my friends made sure to fix me up for the junior and senior proms.

I never got the flirting gene or could even imitate those skills. I was too shy to look a boy in the eye and couldn't come up with the sparkling repartee that some of my friends found so easy. I was equally awkward in class, visibly trembling when I had to read something out loud to fellow students.

By senior year, I was thoroughly bored. I was in so-called honors classes that in my small high school were laughably slow. In my English class, it took all semester for us to read and study three Shakespeare plays. The next year, in a college class, I would read and write papers about three Shakespeare plays a week.

The same high school English teacher chided me when I wrote a paper about some novel and referred to "a callow youth."

"You mean shallow youth," she said. It was obvious that she didn't know callow was a word. I remained silent, as a polite young lady in a small Southern town was wont to do.

I knew I wanted to go to the University of North Carolina, because my parents had attended UNC and I'd always loved the Chapel Hill campus. Besides it had a vaguely raffish reputation as being way too liberal, perhaps even socialist.

Sitting in the family room, I told my mother I'd apply in the fall for early decision to UNC Chapel Hill and wouldn't consider other schools. She was slightly alarmed.

"What if you don't get in?" she asked.

"Then I'll wait and apply again in the spring."

I got in. Finally, I thought, my real life will begin.

CHAPTER 7
WAKING UP TO POSSIBILITY

"A university training is the great ordinary means to a great but ordinary end; it aims at raising the intellectual tone of society...It is the education which gives a man a clear conscious view of his own opinions and judgments, a truth in developing them, an eloquence in expressing them and a force in urging them."
John Henry Newman, *The Idea of a University*

One hot August morning, Daddy, Mother, Jane and I packed up the family station wagon and headed to Chapel Hill. It was a day I'd been anticipating for a year. We were traveling south to the college of my dreams. I was as excited as I've ever been, before or since.

We got to my assigned room in Spencer dormitory and met my roommate, Peggy, a down-home blonde from a small town in Eastern North Carolina. We had written each other already and I felt like I knew her. My parents and Jane helped me unpack, hugged me and left to visit some of my parents' hangouts from their courting days. I was on my own – at last.

Within days of setting foot on the UNC campus, I felt happy – even giddy. I'd been so stifled in high school that my freedom seemed miraculous. I'd gone from a small, conservative town of 10,000 to a university with more than 15,000 students that year. It was also a model of progressive thought with excellent academics.

I felt better about my height, meeting men and women who seemed to genuinely admire my tallness. Also, at a large university, there were a few women who were as tall or even taller. In my high school years, I was usually the tallest student.

Besides, it was easier not to dwell on my height because so many other things were going on in my life. College offered a plethora of choices and benefits.

It was a minor victory just to be allowed to go to Chapel Hill. My mother, who made the college decisions in the family that weren't dictated by money (or the lack of it), felt strongly that girls should be "finished." That is, they should spend two years at a women's college where they'd learn manners and be protected from bad influences, i.e. men.

My older sister attended Longwood College in Farmville, Va. for two years. (The state school was a bargain that helped out my strapped parents, and she couldn't attend the men-only University of Virginia as a freshman.) Two younger sisters went to St. Mary's in Raleigh, N.C. and to Sweet Briar College in rural Virginia. After two years, they all decamped from those single-sex institutions to universities.

I was having none of a women-only college.

I wanted to go to class with men, be around male students and go out with some. After the somnolent atmosphere of high school, I also wanted the most challenging educational environment I could get.

I was very lucky. The fall class of 1967 was only the second year UNC had allowed women to enter as freshmen. Previously, they were allowed to come only as junior transfers.

It was a blessing and a curse – a blessing that I started college at an auspicious time and a curse because both the administration and male students weren't sure what to make of us. Were we early-stage feminists? Were we too brainy to be date-worthy? Many male students still went to the nearby girls' schools to procure dates. Should the university allow us to run as free as the men, or did we need to be protected?

The university, unfortunately for us, still thought we were delicate flowers of the South who needed to be shielded from the free lifestyle of campus life. The dean of women was an older lady whose solemn speeches harked back to the 19th century. Chief among her views – and those of the male administrators who were mostly in charge – was that the university had a duty to act "in loco parentis," in place of our parents.

Policies were gender-based and discriminatory. Female students had to wear skirts or dresses to class. This led to sneaky disobedience, such as women who showed up for 8 a.m. classes in pajamas covered by raincoats.

Even on weekends, female students' curfews were severely limited, and we had to sign out with a front-desk monitor. In our dorm parlor, physical displays of affection (shortened to PDA) with dates were verboten.

We chafed at all of the outdated rules, but none made us more furious than "closed study." Unlike men who roamed the streets of Chapel Hill at any hour, freshman women were confined to their rooms on weeknights from 8 until 10:30 p.m. We were theoretically studying, but because it was so confining, we mostly complained about our plight and didn't get much done.

One night soon after the fall semester began with closed study, I innocently went to the basement vending machine to get a soft drink. One of the resident advisors followed stealthily behind and confronted me.

"You broke closed study," she said triumphantly, a fake look of concern creasing her face.

"I didn't know I couldn't get a Coke," I said, quaking in my bedroom slippers.

"Well, I'll let it pass, just this once," she said.

"Oh, thank you," I said gratefully.

Toward the close of that school year, the deaths of Martin Luther King Jr. and Robert F. Kennedy and other tumultuous events made the ridiculous rules for women look even more trivial and antiquated.

When I came back as a sophomore, due to changing times and some hard work by committed women activists, all of those so-called parietal rules disappeared. Women were treated more on an equal footing to men.

In fact, between 1967-68 and my sophomore year of 1968-69, the university changed in many ways and I changed with it. My freshman year featured fraternity parties where beach bands and Deep South music was often preferred over that of the Beatles and Rolling Stones. Women often got very drunk and a rape incident whispered about in our dorm ended with the departure of a female student. I was careful on the rare occasions I attended those events, (there's nothing scarier than a totally blitzed fraternity guy) and to mostly bypass the garbage cans (clean, I hope!) filled with PJ (Purple Jesus.), a noxious liquor and juice concoction. Sophomore year, I'd start avoiding fraternity parties like poison ivy.

I was fortunate to be assigned to Spencer, the only women's dorm with its own dining room. We had breakfast (excellent) every morning in our robes, where women students could brace themselves for classes or treat hangovers with eggs, bacon and pancakes. A friend of mine once threw up in her eggs after a night of too much partying and too many beers. Needless to say, she was extremely embarrassed, and the kitchen staff was more than disgusted.

My newfound friends, mostly students from larger high schools in North Carolina, were soul mates. They and a few others became almost like sisters. They convinced me that the staid Republicanism of my parents was hopelessly outdated, and I became a committed liberal. Most significantly, we passed up the chance to rush, except for one woman who later joined a coed fraternity. Sororities were experiencing a low point in popularity as student activism increased. They seemed too much like a throwback to the elitist in-crowds of high school life. The *Daily Tar Heel* cartoonists relentlessly lampooned the sillier rituals of sororities and fraternities, so it was easy to reject that part of campus life. At that time, at least one fraternity regularly scheduled "Old South" weekends, where they dressed up as Confederate generals. The Greek life had some ugly and sexist traditions that refused to die.

Several of my new friends were tall and we joked about giving the shorter members of our group "the Redwood treatment." We'd stand around one shorter woman in particular and wave our arms forward while she would recoil in mock fright. It was good for a serious coed like me to laugh about being tall.

My friends and I were self-styled activists, later demonstrating against the Vietnam War, Kent State killings and in support of local issues such as a cafeteria workers' strike for better wages and working conditions. I had my own Chapel Hill world but was part of a more expansive society.

We weren't staid or stuffy. We felt just as much joy as anyone on campus, staying up talking, drinking, joking and seeing how much fun we could wring out of campus life. But we all loved our studies.

My freshman year, I ended up in an accelerated English class of too-aggressive men who'd attended fancy prep schools. When the professor asked a question, a dozen eager hands would go up. Those students tended to give longwinded, self-important answers. I sat in the back of the classroom and hardly ever raised my hand. It would take me a while to feel good about contributing in classes.

Although I was dating pretty regularly, I couldn't seem to find a guy I was really drawn to. Most of them seemed too old-fashioned, taking me to football games and dinners out where women still dressed in new suits and dresses.

That would soon change. In my sophomore year, I'd fall in love and suffer the sublime highs and debilitating lows of a major romance. Again, I'd change in ways I couldn't have foreseen.

CHAPTER 8
TWO PASSIONS, ONE TEMPORARY AND ONE ENDURING

Two of the most significant things that happened during my years at UNC were joining the student newspaper staff and falling in love for the first time. Only one of those passions was to last.

Still shy and lacking in confidence because of my tallness, I surprised myself by walking into the cluttered office of the *Daily Tar Heel* close to the end of my freshman year. There, I found, my height mattered less than the fact that I was a woman in a man's world. The roles of women on the newspaper staff were severely restricted, whether the females were tall or short.

I told the editors, nearly all brash males, that I wanted to be a reporter. I was assigned to the general news pool. Since the assigning editors and most reporters were men, women often got left with stories that were less important. I remember being teased by a male editor who once asked me to sharpen his pencils. (I didn't.) This was 1968, about a year before the women's liberation movement would explode on most campuses throughout the country. It was about time. Sexism was rampant at UNC and certainly on display at the *Daily Tar Heel* offices.

But I was grateful to be given a chance to write, even the not-so-glamorous assignments such as covering minor campus events that usually were published in the paper's back pages. Occasionally, fewer male students showed up for the afternoon shift and I got something meaty, such as interviewing the chancellor. I felt good that I was able to overcome my shyness to interview strangers. Above all, I was proud that it came from my own efforts, not something my mother and father had arranged for me at my father's paper.

Since the newspaper's real work was accomplished roughly between the hours of 3-7 p.m., I didn't have much time for studying on weekdays. I developed a habit of spending all day on Sundays cramming or simply catching up. Often that wasn't enough and if I felt my grades slipping, I'd take a week or two off from the *Tar Heel*. But usually the paper's needs came first, and I resigned myself to imperfect grades. If I kept a grade point average in the A-minus or B-plus range, I felt satisfied.

As I moved into my first journalism classes, I noticed a strange phenomenon. Professors and often students in the J-School disdained the *Tar Heel* as a so-called liberal rag. (The editorials were often audacious or just plain weird. One editor seemed to write editorials only when stoned.) Most of the journalism majors tended to work for the school's monthly publication called the *UNC Journalist*. I wondered how they'd get the experience they needed to get decent internships or practice daily journalism. Besides that, they were missing out on the fun of putting out a daily paper.

The UNC student body elected the *Tar Heel's* editor-in-chief, making it a popularity contest that attracted a motley crew of intelligent, sometimes wildly out of the mainstream, students. I was too intimidated to even think of running, but I worked for several candidates I liked. I was to stay with the paper through my junior year. Senior year I mostly worked on buffing up my grade point average in case I wanted to go to grad school.

I considered my journalism classes, especially the basic required courses like News Writing and News Editing, more workmanlike than inspiring. (The higher-level classes, such as Photography, Feature Writing and International Journalism, were much more fulfilling and taught me more.) But my passion was for English literature, especially small-scale seminars such as one I took on the novels of Anthony Trollope and Henry James. I was influenced by my scholarly friends and knew I could write decent term papers. I once argued with my father, the newspaper editor and publisher, that I could be a perfectly good journalist without majoring in journalism. He pointed out correctly that since UNC had one of the highest-rated journalism schools in the country, I would be foolish to pass up a chance to get a J-School degree. I was to find that he was right – my journalism degree always served me in good stead.

The spring of my sophomore year, I tried out with a few friends for parts in a classic Greek play called *The Bacchae*. The lead, charged with playing the ill-fated god of wine, was a tall, skinny junior named Eric. I didn't get a part, but the director asked me to be part of the lighting crew. During rehearsals, Eric and I became friendly and he asked me out. Soon we started dating and he said rather prematurely that he was falling in love with me. I was taken aback because I wasn't that sure of my feelings for him.

He appreciated my height, though, especially my long legs and short skirts. I was flattered enough to ignore the fact that I was moving into a relationship I wasn't really sure about. We were both needy in different ways.

One day, as we shared a forbidden kiss in the Spencer parlor, he surprised me with his fervent declaration.

"I love you, I love you, I love you," he said. "Do you love me?"

I hesitated. "I'm concerned about your welfare." My stiff answer became a running joke with us.

I'd never dated anyone like Eric. That wasn't even his name; he used it instead of his real name. This was a telling clue to his personality. He was a typical actor, flamboyant, overly dramatic and emotional. He occasionally cried when he was drunk or disappointed by a friend. And he didn't have many friends, which seemed odd.

His parents, both New York transplants, also seemed strange and somewhat remote to me. They'd brought their only child to North Carolina for a more prosperous life but hadn't fully accepted the Southern culture. The oddest thing about them was their love for their pet monkey. The smelly spider monkey, fondly known as Muncharoony, lived mostly in his dining room cage, but was occasionally allowed the run of the house. One time he put a paw into my wine glass, which I found disgusting.

Eric's intense feelings for me eventually won me over and by the summer, we were sending daily adoring letters between Durham and Suffolk, Va., where my parents had moved for my father's new job as editor and publisher of the *Suffolk News-Herald*. I'd come home for lunch from my job as a reporter for my dad's paper and there would usually be a letter waiting for me on the hall table.

My parents, especially my mother, disapproved of this daily correspondence and didn't encourage visits. But they grudgingly agreed he could come once to Suffolk so they could look him over. Predictably they disliked him. Eric was very intelligent, but kind of a bombastic showoff. My mother, ever the Southern lady, was suspicious of his Yankee background.

The clearest memory I have of Eric's trip to see me in Suffolk is my mother's lecture about us walking down Main Street holding hands. She discouraged public displays of affection. I remember a lot of strained conversations between Eric and my parents, who didn't know what to make of his theatrical personality and passion for acting.

I knew in my heart that we didn't quite work as a couple but wouldn't admit it because I was so flattered by his devotion. My junior year we picked out a sapphire ring and told our parents we were engaged. Furthermore, we planned to be married that summer.

After much discussion with my parents, our engagement was announced in my dad's paper. Then I started to think that maybe I'd be making a huge mistake to marry Eric or anyone else so quickly. My whole life was ahead of me and I'd essentially move from my parents' house to my husband's apartment. I'd be missing out on my last carefree year of college. My doubts took over and I refused to set a wedding date. But somehow, I wasn't confident enough to break it off. My procrastination resulted in an engagement visit to Suffolk by Eric's parents that summer to look at wedding venues, every bit as awkward as it sounds.

Toward the end of the weekend, we got a chance to walk in my parents' backyard where the summer flowers bloomed. I told him I really didn't want to get married, that I thought we were too young, and our personalities were too different. We both cried, and he said he'd tell his parents on their way back to Durham. My relief lasted the rest of the summer.

Though Eric and I would resume dating for a while my senior year, it was basically out of misplaced habit. The thrill was gone, and we broke up for good before the year was over. I never saw his parents or their stinky monkey again.

CHAPTER 9
A LIFELONG ROLE MODEL

I spent several summers during my college years working as a reporter for my father's paper. It taught me plenty of life lessons, particularly by observing my father and the way he did business.

My father never chose his job. In his many attempts to get stable employment after World War II, he stumbled into journalism.

After a stint in advertising and running a weekly, he was successively the editor and publisher of two small Virginia newspapers owned by a chain of small publications. As I've mentioned, the first was located in Radford in southwest Virginia and the second was in Suffolk, in the state's coastal area. Circulation was modest – about 5,000 subscriptions at most.

My life was inextricably bound to those newspapers. My first real job was proofreading the Radford paper the summer I was 14. I'd sit in a dingy office in the basement near the printing presses and workers would bring me freshly inked galleys – long columns of print – to read. I'd mark them up with the proofreading symbols I had learned. I was proud that I could spot errors quickly. The job had long hours, but I loved it because I was working with my father. He'd discuss his day during our rides home for lunch and dinner, almost as one adult to another.

When we walked down the street together, we were almost of equal height (he was only an inch taller) and people said we had the same familiar lope of a tall person who doesn't stand up straight enough.

The summer I was 19 and a prospective sophomore at UNC, I started working as a reporter at his Suffolk paper, soaking in the art and craft of newspapering. I covered mostly city council and police news. I'd observe the honorable, friendly way my father dealt with employees, customers, advertising prospects and anyone else who came in the door. He even delivered newspapers after hours to customers who'd call us at home to say they hadn't gotten one. He worked incredible hours to keep the business going, wrote pithy editorials and sometimes shot pictures and wrote high school football stories.

My dad never got a journalism degree or even finished college. He had to leave UNC to serve in the Navy during World War II. I admired him for all he had managed to learn on his own. His editorials particularly were so good they won awards from the state press association.

His proficiencies cemented my desire to be a journalist, but I never wanted to work for a small paper. You were basically forced into doing things you weren't good at, like taking pictures and writing headlines. My ambition was to work for large newspapers where my stories reached a lot of readers and really made a difference.

For my father, journalism was changing, in ways that boded ill for today's industry. In the early 1980s, he was rewarded for decades of loyalty by being laid off from his mercenary chain. He was a few years short of retirement age, but a new generation owned the newspapers and the ungrateful son wanted to get rid of the old guys. My father negotiated a settlement and eventually wrote columns for the new editor. I treasure those folksy columns. My dad died in 1995 and I lost the best role model I ever had.

When I think of opinion leaders referring to the media as "an enemy of the people," I'm offended. I wonder if citizens understand how diligently journalists work to bring the truth to light. I've never met a reporter who didn't take the work seriously, who didn't wake up in the middle of the night worrying about misspelling a name or who didn't put in extra hours to ensure a story was airtight.

My father devoted his life to tough jobs in the trenches. I lived by his example and still feel that journalism is a sacred calling.

CHAPTER 10
THE INFLUENCE OF A STRONG WOMAN

My mother always pressed me to be a writer. She assumed I'd follow in my father's footsteps and be a journalist. She was pleased as I became a reporter for larger publications. She subscribed to the papers I worked for and read some of the most boring stories I wrote. But that wasn't enough. She said she always knew I could write a book.

I guess her belief in me paid off. I was a journalist for 38 years. After I retired, I wrote two novels. She was complimentary, to a point. She said the books contained far too much sex and violence. Still, she told me she was proud of me and invited me to her book club twice to talk about them.

As you can guess, my mother was the major influence in my life. My father was my role model for getting along with people and succeeding in journalism through hard work. My mother showed me how to get things done by sheer force of will.

She would do anything for her five children, but she also expected them to unquestionably accept her guidance. This was where our relationship often ran into trouble. Though my career choices mirrored her suggestions, she often didn't like other decisions, such as some boyfriends I had, my propensity for freewheeling travel and my short skirts.

Despite our occasional inability to get along, I loved her desperately and I knew that the love was returned in full force. When she died on December 6, 2018, I mourned without ceasing. I still can't accept my status as a motherless child. Sometimes I think for a fleeting moment that she'll telephone me, or I should call her.

My mother was nonchalant about my height, helping me to find dresses and skirts that were long enough. She never said anything that indicated she wished I was shorter. Even when I was 13 or 14 and at my most unattractive (family pictures don't lie), she just told me, and all of her girls, to put on more lipstick. Consequently, I'm always refreshing my lipstick.

It was about that time that my PE class was learning modern dance. I was stunningly bad at it and Mrs. Sandidge, our teacher, suggested to me that I was awkward because of my height. I told my mother and the next day, she went to give the teacher a piece of her mind. I'm not sure what was said, but Mrs. Sandidge treated me with kid gloves the rest of the year.

The incident was illustrative of my ambivalence toward my mother's Mama-bear personality. I loved it when it was aimed at my enemies but disliked it when it landed on me. For instance, she didn't like my 1960s thrift-shop jeans and thought I should be dressing in a more ladylike way. I ignored that bit of advice.

Like all people, my mother had her quirks, but even those seemed larger than life. She never got over being a Southern belle and worrying about her looks. She was beautiful as a shapely young woman, but also as a ninety-something elderly lady. With her white-blonde hair, blue eyes and up-to-the-minute clothes, she elicited compliments practically every time we went out, even in the last decade of her life. She loved the attention.

One time when I felt that she'd talked too long about her college-era boyfriends and which ones her mother and father liked, I asked her why she didn't reminisce about her life as a young mother. In other words, I told her, I wanted to know more about me and what I was like as a child.

She said I was cute, "always dancing around."

Then she paused for a moment and said of her young married life, "It was hard, really hard. You children were sick all the time."

My mother loved to get out with friends, shop and take vacations.

She and I went on hundreds of shopping trips over the years. When she came to Charlotte, she wanted to buy clothes at Chico's and jewelry and shoes at Belk. We spent most of our time together shopping, which was usually fun.

When I went away to college, the youngest child was only four. When Jane started school, my mother had time on her hands. I was glad when she started teaching elementary-age children. She needed an outlet for that prodigious energy. She taught mostly African American students for 25 years and they seemed to love her. She was proud of them when they did something good that made the local newspaper. She was pleased when one former student became a successful entrepreneur and gave out free turkeys to the poor at Christmas. She was always running into former students, who greeted her effusively. Since she had grown up in a nearly all-white part of Tennessee, I admired her lack of prejudice as a teacher.

As children, we took an annual beach vacation, mostly to Florida where my father could trade newspaper advertising for rooms. I both loved these trips and dreaded them. My sisters and I would be crowded in one room, I'd end up with a painful sunburn and got tired of the beach after a few days. But my mother cherished them. She joked that just thinking about them got her through some rough winters.

Because she'd rather be out doing something, my mother wasn't an enthusiastic cook, but I loved her biscuits, cornbread and apple pie. I learned to cook for our family of seven at an early age and I still would rather cook for a crowd than just my husband and myself.

Diane and I always wondered about her desire to have five children. Mother told me all were planned with the exception of the much-cherished lone male, Steve. She said she really wanted six kids but ran out of time before she achieved that goal. In the late 1940's and 1950's, a large family was much more desirable than it would be after the launching of the women's movement.

After my father died in 1995, I was pleased when she found someone to love and marry in Suffolk. Peter was a multi-millionaire and could fully indulge her love of shopping. They had a contented eight years together before he passed away.

Generous by nature and always looking for a tax break, Peter allowed my mother to help establish a network of scholarships at colleges in Virginia and North Carolina. Their names live on in the dozen or so scholarships they set up.

My mother was my best advocate. She was jubilant when I won awards and excited when I got front-page stories. Twice I won the National Press Club's Consumer Journalism Award. She and my father drove eight hours to Washington D.C. to be in the audience while I sat at the head table. When I got close to winning a Pulitzer Prize, according to a colleague who had heard the deliberations, both my parents were wildly excited. Even though I didn't win, they cherished everything about my stories.

I still can't believe my two-person cheering squad is gone.

CHAPTER 11
SCOTCH EGGS AND PORK AND BEANS

As my senior year at the UNC Chapel Hill ground down, I'd done nothing about getting a job.

For most of my last year, I had dithered. I was still dating Eric, my former fiancé, and still refusing to commit to marrying him. I felt stymied. That ended a few months before graduation when we finally broke up for good.

I sat in a popular student bar with a dorm buddy one afternoon and talked about my lack of post-graduation plans.

"Want to go to Europe with me?" She asked.

"You mean it? That sounds great."

My friend wanted to travel with a female friend to please her parents, but also to rendezvous in England with a boyfriend who was studying in Germany.

I wanted to get over my disastrous romance and postpone adulthood for a few months longer. We would both benefit from this inspired idea.

That six-week trip, to London, Paris, Dublin, Florence and Lausanne, Switzerland, changed my sense of the world. I reveled in the freedom of hitchhiking (My friend and I felt safe because we were traveling with a man), staying in bare-bones hostels and going wherever the mood took us.

We flew to Iceland, refueled and landed in Luxembourg, which was the cheapest way to fly in the summer of 1971. Foreign travel was expensive and still rare. I think we paid close to $500 each for tickets, a small fortune then for impoverished students. I had saved enough money from the previous summer's work to be able to afford a very modest trip.

Flying wasn't common in middle-class families in the early 1970s, but I'd been on a plane before. My publisher father had traded some newspaper advertising for a short Piedmont Airlines flight for the family to Myrtle Beach, S.C. This flight, of course, was much longer. I looked down before we landed in Iceland for a refueling stop and all I could see was dull brown land, not an auspicious introduction to my first foreign country.

To my surprise, I found that my height was a boon on this trip. Because I was tall and sturdily built (I'd gained weight in college and looked slim but not skinny), I felt brave enough to hitchhike with friends and safe enough to meet strangers without fear. Being tall made me feel less vulnerable in potentially hazardous situations. It sounds foolhardy now, but in the early 1970s, adventures like hitchhiking and backpacking seemed harmless. My height also brought what I realized were admiring glances from tall European and Scandinavian men. However, I wasn't prepared for Italian men on trains who pressed close to female bodies and pinched our posteriors.

In those days, a trip to Europe was considered exotic. At that time, no one in my family had been abroad, except my father during wartime, and my mother's anxiety was profound. She warned me about such bizarre dangers as a plague of vipers in Florence. (Apparently, she read a news story detailing a bumper season for snakes in Italy.)

My father thought my trip was novel enough to ask me for stories that he used in the newspaper. I suspect he also wanted me to practice journalism before I got rusty, in preparation for job hunting.

Though it was interesting and fun, the European adventure wasn't easy. That first night in suburban London, we arrived close to 11 p.m. and couldn't rouse our hosts, who lived on the second floor of a bakery that was closed. We threw pebbles at the upstairs windows where our friends lived, to no avail. Undaunted, we crossed the street to a deserted park and slept with our heads on our baggage until 6 a.m., when the first coffee shop opened.

I had brought a small canvas suitcase in lieu of a backpack. I remember taking a striped cotton skirt, some tops, some green denim striped pants and a polyester orange dress. I ditched the dress when I bought a leather skirt in Italy. I still have my little suitcase.

Hitchhiking was difficult, especially in Ireland in the days of "The Troubles," the ongoing civil war between Irish factions in the North and South. Apparently, hitchhikers sometimes smuggled arms across the country, so the authorities regarded them with suspicion. We had little luck getting rides. In England, lorry drivers who seemed curious and happy for the company of young Americans had picked us up. Not so in Ireland. After one particularly long day, we were frustrated and angry. My friend was so irritated that she pulled out our cartons of yogurt and splattered them on the pavement. I was too taken aback to say anything to her.

Eating yogurt and English staples like Bubble and Squeak (a fried mixture of cabbage and potatoes) were firsts for me. Because of our lean budgets, we mostly dined on bread, cheese, cereal and other cheap provisions we could carry. But we sometimes chose to splurge on pub food like Scotch Eggs (sausage wrapped around boiled eggs.)

We stayed at low-cost youth hostels, which were mostly crowded and noisy. Once we slept on the floor of a bathroom and awoke to the hostel's less-than-delicious breakfast offering – pork and beans on toast. The hostels ran the gamut from a faded villa in Florence that once belonged to Mussolini's mistress to a rundown house in Ireland where the crazy manager locked all the women in for the night. It was a treat to hear different languages and see different groups of mostly young people traveling from all over the world.

There was a bit of romance as well. I spent an afternoon on a riverbank with a tall Dutch guy where we kissed in lieu of our inability to speak much of the same language.

The scenery was often beautiful but sometimes as mundane as anything I'd seen in backwoods North Carolina. We thrilled to Westminster Abbey in London and the pristine buildings on the Seine in Paris, but also saw a lot of shoddy areas with cheap stores and hotels.

The trip cured me of the myth that the United States was the only country in which I could comfortably live. There were plenty of other places in the world that were lovely, interesting and hospitable to Americans. I could grow and thrive anywhere I chose. I'd always been told that America was the world's greatest country. Now I began to question that jingoistic view. I also developed a lifelong taste for adventure that would serve me well in later years when I could afford to travel widely.

And I learned the value of team effort. My two friends turned out to be resourceful problem solvers. We relied on each other to navigate the problems of getting around on a tight budget. People sometimes stared at us, wondering why one man was traveling with two women. On the rare occasions when we stayed at a hotel instead of a hostel, all three of us crowded into the same room.

Since I was essentially a third wheel on the trip, I sometimes felt lonely and wondered whether I'd done the right thing to break up with Eric. I worried about ever finding a suitable mate. But as the trip wore on, I felt better about my prospects as a single.

By the time we returned, I felt confident of my ability to adapt to most situations – and to my surprise, my tallness had contributed to a sense of well-being.

But I hadn't yet experienced the challenges of job hunting and living without the safety net of dorm life.

My father was eager to get me off the payroll and make financial room for the next sibling to go to college, so he took my feeble efforts to find a job seriously. We talked about it at the kitchen table, where it seemed, most decisions of consequence were made.

"I heard they're looking for someone in Charlottesville. Do you want to give the editor a call?"

"Sure, I guess so," I told him.

I was less than enthusiastic about working for the skinflint newspaper chain that employed my father. I knew I would make very little money and the *Daily Progress*, the newspaper in Charlottesville, Va, didn't strike me as interesting or likely to advance my journalism career.

But I didn't have any other immediate prospects, so I went for an interview with the managing editor. I immediately disliked his slick personality and the cheap look of the ancient newsroom with its wooden desks and bad chairs.

"We really need a women's editor," he said. "Are you interested?"

"Oh, definitely," I said with as much enthusiasm as I could muster.

In reality, my heart sank. I didn't want to be a women's editor at all. I hated the thought of writing up weddings, parties and coverage of what were considered female topics. I wanted to cover big news stories. But that was the only job offer I had, and my poor father needed me gone.

"When can I start?"

CHAPTER 12
MY FIRST FULL TIME JOB

Could I have had a worse first fulltime journalism job? I didn't think so. I spent nearly a year as women's editor of the *Daily Progress* in Charlottesville. I ended up hating the newspaper, its bosses and most of all, the job. And I fell in love again – with someone who didn't appreciate my tallness.

I enjoyed living in Charlottesville, a beautiful college town of a manageable size, a vibrant downtown and the attractions of the University of Virginia. I loved the hills and the Blue Ridge Mountains to the west of the city. Whenever I was particularly unhappy, I'd drive half an hour to the top of majestic Afton Mountain southwest of the city. I was soothed by the wonderful views and happy to drive back to my apartment just a few miles from Mr. Jefferson's University.

I shared a $230-a-month new apartment with a grad student who was looking for a roommate. It was a good arrangement for both of us.

Since my salary was a princely $115 a week, I could barely afford to share that nice place.

My friend (for she quickly became my friend) had a boyfriend and they did wholesome things together like go to a group singing performance of "The Messiah." In contrast, I felt like my own social life was mostly a mess.

The most I can say about that year-long experience is that I found out a lot about myself, what I liked and didn't like and how easy it was to make mistakes on the job.

I also learned a lot of fundamental facts about the newspaper business. Your time is not your own. You work until the job is done and you spend a lot of holidays in the newsroom. That year, after deadline, a copy editor kindly invited the young people on Thanksgiving duty to a late dinner at his home. It was the first Thanksgiving I'd ever had away from my family.

My bosses' vision of my job and my own concept were vastly at odds. Charlottesville and the bucolic towns around it attracted a lot of retirees and rich people who drew a line at mixing with common townies, especially those involved in journalism. My bosses wanted me to penetrate and report on the world of the wealthy – and snobbish. At the time, Lynda Bird Johnson lived with her law student husband at an exclusive gated community with other bright lights of the social world. As a proud college lefty and near-hippie, I found the expectations intolerable. I didn't object to reporting on women. I just wanted to interview and write about women who were actually doing something interesting. In the early days of the feminist movement, women were beginning to be elected to office, fill government positions and chosen for other leadership roles. In addition, the Charlottesville area attracted plenty of artists and writers, women I loved meeting and writing about. The bosses wanted weddings, fancy parties and tidbits about the rich and famous. I wanted to focus on women more involved in the world around them. At 22, I wasn't interested in babies, cooking or other housewifely pursuits that were still believed to be the domain of women. I always seemed to be on the edge of job trouble and felt grossly inadequate to satisfy the editors.

My supervisor had the habit of coming by my desk with unwelcome suggestions for society coverage.

"Hey, there's some kind of charity event at Farmington Country Club," he said one day. "Why don't you go check it out?"

I groaned to myself but went to the boring event. Women were dressed to the hilt and I was wearing one of the few inexpensive dresses I had bought for my job. I was snubbed until the women found out I was a newspaper reporter. Then I was welcomed with open arms.

On another occasion, a top editor ripped up the front of the Sunday women's section that prominently featured my long interview with a female mayor in a nearby town.

"This is too much," he said with disgust. "We need other stuff on the page too."

If memory serves, he slapped a few recipes and homemaking tips on the revised page. He pointedly did not ask my opinion.

The only saving grace to the job was that I didn't have to write up the wedding stories. The newsroom clerk performed that odious task, using a strict template that left no room for individuality. That was before I started reading the *New York Times* wedding coverage and realized that such news could be interesting.

The newsroom had a coterie of young reporters, mostly women who could be persuaded to work at low pay and long hours. They became my friends and voiced many of the same frustrations, but their jobs weren't as likely to cause conflict. They covered city councils, school boards, police departments and other government beats. I was glad to have some kindred spirits with which to go to lunch and complain about the limitations of the newsroom.

I dated a lot that year – a would-be poet, a younger student from UNC and a man who claimed to work for the CIA. (Well, he did seem to have advance knowledge that the Vietnam War was drawing to a close.)

None shattered my confidence as a tall woman until I dated the son of the chief executive officer of a Charlottesville business. Gary worked at the newspaper as an advertising salesman, a job that particularly suited his slick, outgoing personality. He was conventionally handsome and subtly let me know I wasn't attractive enough to meet his usual standards. He had dark hair and a physique that had been toned by a stint in the U.S Army. He was the kind of young, good-looking man who flirted with nearly every woman he met. His nearly nude pictures of one woman caused the guy who ran the paper's photography studio to blush with embarrassment when he printed them.

He was hardly my usual type, but I fell for him and he fell for me, despite what he viewed as my unattractive height and lack of good looks. Given my shaky self-confidence, I was flattered that such a handsome man would pay attention to me. It was akin to the star of the football team noticing the homely girl on the sidelines of the dance. I mistook his domineering attitude as self-assurance instead of self-centeredness.

I possessed no athletic ability, which as a frat-boy type, he scorned. One Saturday morning, he persuaded me to go to a park to shoot baskets with him. I dressed in shorts with my long hair piled up in a baseball cap and a loose T-shirt hiding any curves on my angular body. A man passing by greeted us with friendly words.

"Hey, guys," he said. "Great day for basketball."

Gary looked at me with shock.

"Damn it, I can't believe it. He thought you were a man."

That incident bothered him greatly and made me even more self-conscious about my tallness. He was accustomed to towering over women and felt diminished by dating a female just his height.

Still, the relationship sputtered along, and we even talked about marriage. (However, I had escaped one marriage trap and was more than leery about entering into another flawed engagement.) Luckily for me, his proven ability to sell advertising got him the top job at a smaller newspaper in rural Tennessee. I visited him once in his trailer park home (the small town had little appropriate housing for a rising young bachelor) and we broke up. True to his history, while I was there, a woman actually showed up at his door to borrow sugar.

It had been awkward to date the son of a CEO. His parents were unwelcoming, and I felt that my height coupled with my shyness made me undesirable to them. They were apparently used to Gary dating petite prom queens, not a six-foot, gangly girl whose lack of confidence was apparent in social situations.

After the breakup with Gary and increasing tension with my editor, I'd had enough of Charlottesville and my disappointing job. I felt bad that my work with my father's penny-pinching chain hadn't exactly covered me – or by extension, him – with glory. My dad deserved better than a rebellious daughter who challenged authority and often ignored what she was told to do.

I began applying to newspapers in Virginia and North Carolina, papers that were larger with higher journalism aspirations than the *Progress*.

In July, eleven months after I started the ill-fated job, I got an offer from the *Times-Herald* in Newport News, Va. It was a much bigger paper with better management. They hired me as a general assignment reporter. No more women's news and obnoxious assignments to profile social movers and shakers.

I sat at my parents' kitchen table one weekend to talk to them about my new job. My newspaper editor father was dubious.

"You should have given it more time. You don't want to be known a job hopper," he said disapprovingly.

"It's a better job that will be a step up in my career," I said.

"But you've only been at your first job for less than a year."

"I don't care. It's been a terrible year and a horrible job."

In contrast to my father and his misgivings, my mother was jubilant.

"She'll be a lot closer, less than an hour away from us," she said. "And Newport News is a nice town."

In the end, I think my father understood.

I couldn't get out of Charlottesville fast enough.

CHAPTER 13
A SHORTER MAN

One night in October 1973, I stood in my apartment kitchen at a party I was giving, talking with one of the most intelligent and interesting men I'd ever met. He was also very handsome, with dark hair, brown eyes and a way of focusing in on me during our conversation.

The catch? Len Norman was about two inches shorter than me, about 5-foot-10. Being just shy of six feet had given me the lifelong habit of quickly sizing up people's heights, especially those of men.

What a pity, I thought. Growing up tall in the 1960s meant I automatically accepted the social constructs of the time, which were rigid and unforgiving. I'd seen plenty of cartoons making fun of women who loomed over shorter men. I'd read advice columns where women who actually dated shorter men bemoaned the height difference.

In one study, a 6-foot-1 man said his ideal female would be 5-foot-3 and "dependent on me at all times." Another college male in the study said his ideal mate would be a 5-foot-2 woman "who is simple and doesn't ask a lot of questions."

In my own experience, shorter men had asked me out fairly often, seeing me as a kind of vertical challenge, I guess. I usually turned them down. The taller men seemed to be drawn toward the shorter women. It was unfair.

I was living in Newport News in the Tidewater area of Virginia. My latest job had led me to a newspaper and work that I loved. But it was in a blue-collar city where shipbuilding and military bases reigned. Most of the single, younger men I'd met were less educated and didn't share my progressive views. I'd dated a few and could easily predict that we'd have little in common.

Len, a University of Virginia graduate a few months older than me, was different. He worked as a city planner and we shared similar views about the world. We'd each grown up with four siblings in conventional, middle-class households where education was important. Unlike me, he was calm and practical. He reminded me somewhat of my dad.

Still, I turned him down when he called twice for dates. I was seeing someone else semi-seriously and the height difference still seemed like a barrier.

But the relationship with the other boyfriend petered out after a few months and I found myself single again. One dateless Friday night, my newspaper friend Mary Anne convinced me to attend a local Sierra Club meeting where Len was speaking. He impressed me with his quiet authority and lack of self-importance. After the meeting, he and one of his friends asked Mary Anne and me to his apartment for a beer. We quickly agreed.

I walked into Len's ground-floor apartment and was surprised to see a single man's lair that was neat, uncluttered and nicely appointed. Even on a city planner's budget, he'd made it warm and inviting. It had a nice green striped couch, a matching chair and a handsome bookcase he'd fashioned from an original design of wooden squares.

We sat in the living room, had a few beers and some relaxed conversation. Len and his friend regaled us with city planning successes and failures. We said goodbye after a couple of hours and agreed it had been a fun evening.

The next morning, my phone rang. It was Len.

"I know it's kind of last-minute, but would you like to go to a Christmas party tonight? One of my neighbors is giving it," he said.

"Sure, that sounds like fun."

I enjoyed his company at the festive event and the easy, friendly way he related to the guests and hostess. One of the men attending paid a little too much attention to me, but Len took it in stride.

It was the start of the kind of romance I hadn't had before. The love we soon felt for each other was grounded in respect and liking. I had loved both Eric and Gary, but those relationships had been flawed and destined to fail. This was different. Len said he liked me for my intelligence as well as my looks. As a tall woman, I'd been looking for unconditional acceptance all my life. He seemed happy with my personality and wasn't cowed by my height. He said he was seeking a union of equals. It felt like the real thing.

We dated for more than two years as both of us grew into our careers and into the relationship. My parents, who'd been unimpressed by boyfriends Eric and Gary, liked Len and often invited us to their home in Suffolk.

I covered a lot of night meetings for my newspaper in Newport News and Len would often fix me dinner beforehand or I'd stop for a beer afterwards. He made great home-cooked meals of macaroni and cheese, paella and other offerings from "Cooking for Two," the recipe book his mother had given him.

One night I entered his apartment to the delicious smell of meat baking.

"Something smells really great. What're you cooking?"

"It's Swiss steak, one of my favorites."

The casserole-like dish consisted of round steak, tomatoes, cheese and spices. We sat at his small table and enjoyed every bit.

"You got the recipe from your mother's cookbook?"

"Oh yeah," he said. "I'm not one of those guys who eats out of cans or makes some kind of slop that lasts all week.

"It's not that hard to cook yourself a decent meal," he added.

I could tell that he was no stranger to housekeeping either. He vacuumed, dusted and cleaned regularly.

"Unlike with other guys I've dated, I'm not afraid to go into your bathroom," I said.

"That's good. I'm not going to live like a slob."

We talked about marriage occasionally, but I was wary. My two previous serious relationships had made me skittish of a long-term commitment. I'd had a recurring dream where I'd walk down the aisle in my wedding finery and was shocked to find a coffin at the front of the church. That nightmare didn't inspire confidence.

We developed a nice circle of friends, mostly newspaper colleagues with whom we'd enjoy crabbing, the beach and other water-related activities. Len and I spent time mostly at my place, but we kept separate households. My parents were just an hour away, and it was before living together was common, even among serious couples.

During the nearly four years at the *Times-Herald*, I came more into my own as a news reporter. Covering municipal and county government, including crime, taxes, courts, sewer systems and other unglamorous but necessary topics, was good training. I had an excellent editor and female mentor. Myrtle, a large woman with a big heart and a passion for local reporting, was an exacting boss. She was an officer in the Virginia Press Women, and she persuaded most of the other women in the newsroom to join that lively group.

One day she called me into a quiet office. I felt nervous. But she made a surprising offer.

"I'm pleased with your growth as a writer," she said. "I'd like you to be our special assignments reporter, to cover big events and explore bigger stories in the region."

"I'd love to do that," I said, envisioning fewer night meetings and riveting governmental discussions about cable TV franchises, garbage pickup and litter control.

That ushered in a year of interesting projects like why the downtown area was declining and how it might be rejuvenated and how a giant new project called Busch Gardens would transform Colonial Williamsburg.

My editor also sent me to cover heads of state when they made brief appearances in Williamsburg, ranging from Emperor Hirohito of Japan to King Carl Gustav, the newly crowned heir to the Swedish throne. Since relatively little news actually came out of those visits, I learned ways to describe mood, atmosphere and facial expressions.

At the same time, Len began to get restive with city planning work. He'd prepare great plans that never had a chance of being implemented. He decided he'd work toward getting his master's in business administration. He applied to a top school, Stanford University, and got in. Suddenly, getting married became more than theoretical.

One night we sat on his deck for a serious conversation about it.

"Why can't we just live together?" I said, spooked by the thought of another engagement.

"Since I'm going to California for two years, we should either commit or go our separate ways." I was surprised at his serious tone. I didn't want to lose the best boyfriend I'd ever had.

"Okay," I finally said. "Let's get married, but not make too big a fuss about it."

"We could get married at the city jail," he said. The jail building housed the justice of the peace offices.

"Are you kidding? That would be awful."

That made up my mind to have a small wedding and we had the quickest engagement and speediest nuptials of any of my friends. My mother planned it all while I finished out the remaining projects in my newspaper job. I went out and bought a Victorian styled, long white cotton dress for $50 and the men rented white tuxes. I asked to be married at my parents' home, but my mother nixed that idea.

"You have to get married in a church." She said she'd be scandalized if we didn't. We acceded to her wishes and my parents agreed to hold the reception at their home.

We only invited about fifty people, mostly relatives and our closest friends, so the church that seated hundreds looked rather bare. After the noon ceremony, my parents hosted a nice brunch. It was sweltering on August 14, 1976, and our guests ate chicken salad and guzzled champagne on the back porch. Our honeymoon was a few days at my parents' Kill Devil Hills, N.C. beach cottage just two hours away.

I stopped noticing that he was a few inches shorter. Marrying Len, which changed my life in so many ways, was the best decision I ever made.

CHAPTER 14
GOLDEN AND WACKY

From the sofa in our second-floor apartment in Palo Alto, we had the perfect view of a large avocado tree. We watched it hungrily.

One warm afternoon, the biggest avocado I'd ever seen dropped from the tree. Len raced out to get it.

"A few more of these and we'll have guacamole," he said, displaying the shiny green fruit. The avocado tree was a marvel to us, just like our new life in Northern California.

Living in the San Francisco Bay area would mean waking every day to something beautiful, surprising or just plain odd. It was so different from the places we'd lived on the East Coast. Palo Alto was 3,000 miles away from prosaic working-class Newport News. It felt like another planet.

First, we had to make the coast-to-coast pilgrimage to the Golden State.

When Len proposed early in 1976 and we decided to get married and move to the West Coast, I told him I had one condition. As we sat in my apartment one night, I came up with a request that he still laughs about.

"Promise me we'll never live in Des Moines."

He promised, but asked me what I had against Des Moines, a place neither of us had ever visited.

"It's just so landlocked. I can't stand the thought of being that closed in."

The Bay area where we were moving was the antithesis of Des Moines. Dramatic ocean views were so prevalent they couldn't be avoided, even if one wanted to.

Traveling so far in two vehicles was an adventure, one we still talk about with fondness. From our short, cheap honeymoon on the Outer Banks at my parents' cottage, we went for quick goodbye visits to Len's parents in South Carolina, where they were vacationing, and to see a few other relatives in Georgia and Tennessee. Then we got going on the arduous cross-country trip.

That was, of course, before the advent of cell phones, so we followed each other closely and tried to be observant. Len was in the lead and looked for my hand signals.

I'd wave, point or pass him to indicate that I wanted to stop. The days were long and sometimes boring.

My mother had offered to buy us citizen band radios, then popular with truckers, but we declined. It was a strange trip by myself in the little blue Toyota Corolla, but as a newlywed moving across the country, I had a lot to think about. Len had bought a second-hand, turquoise Chevy van, into which we'd squeezed a few pieces of furniture and the carefully edited household items we'd need for our new life.

Many of my thoughts turned to Len and the fact that he'd married me despite the fact that I was two inches taller. I felt lucky to have him.

He'd told me that one of his friends said he must prefer tall women to be dating me.

"I just like Nancy," he said.

The long trip predictably worried my mother and she expressed opinions about every detail.

"Brother says you should definitely take Interstate 40," she said. "It's the safest. You need to listen to Brother."

Brother was my Uncle Frank, an insurance executive who traded in his Cadillac each year for a newer model and drove across country often, even into Canada and Mexico. He never took planes.

We followed Brother's route, which turned out to be safe, but mostly flat and uninspiring. We drove through parts of Tennessee, Arkansas, Arizona, New Mexico and Texas before getting to the desert parts of California.

Still, it was fascinating to see new places and new states during that trip, which lasted nearly a week. Fort Smith, Arkansas, looked homey but homely, the hills of Albuquerque were steep and inviting and radio stations offering Native America music and news enlivened our drive through Arizona.

Texas was the most memorable, however, because there was so much of it. West Texas had a landmark restaurant that drew our curiosity on one of our lunch breaks.

"Let's stop at the Big Texan tonight," Len said. "It's pretty famous. If you eat a 72-ounce steak, you get it free."

"Probably you also get a lot of indigestion."

We didn't order the massive steak but enjoyed the delicious meat and the cowboy atmosphere. We talked about the loneliness of West Texas, its miles and miles of flat land, oil-pumping machinery and tumbleweeds.

We made it eventually to Palo Alto, where even in 1976, housing was incredibly expensive. What we could afford on Len's college savings and my expectations of finding a newspaper job was a dated apartment complex called Tan Village (named after its owner, Mr. Tan.)

It was close to Highway 101, one of the main arteries to San Francisco, so we figured it would be convenient. It had two bedrooms, a living room, a tiny kitchen, hideous olive-brownish carpeting and a small patio. The nights were mostly too cold to relax on the patio.

Len was soon embroiled in a punishing school schedule while I began an arduous search for a job. He found that he was one of just a few Southerners in his class and he worried that his cohorts would see him as stupid, bigoted or worse. We talked about it one night and I tried to reassure him.

You're just as smart and sophisticated as they are, I said. Stop running yourself down.

There were so many would-be journalists in that highly educated part of California that there were seldom any vacancies at the papers in the region. I tried all the dailies and couldn't find anything, though I got good feedback on my clips.

The best thing I could find within a few months was proofreading at a textbook publishing house. This job wasn't just reading often-boring textbooks; it was measuring lines between sentences and paying attention to fonts and headlines. I worked the 3-11 p.m. shift. I had two coworkers I liked a lot; an older lady named Kaye, and Bob, a young man about my age.

But the job felt temporary and I could see trouble ahead when there were fewer books to edit. One night my editor gave me my paycheck, saying, "This is the last one."

That was a heck of a way to lay someone off and I insisted on a conversation that salved my wounded ego. It wasn't me, he said. I was just the last one hired.

Bob came back to the house to meet Len and have a farewell drink. He looked around the Spartan apartment and said, "You could definitely cut back. This is a palace."

Of course, we could tell that he was vastly relieved he wasn't the one laid off.

CHAPTER 15
ITALIANS AND HELL'S ANGELS

Pete Seeger, in his famous song *Little Boxes*, wrote about houses on a hillside "made of ticky-tacky... there's a green one and a pink one and a blue one and a yellow one ... And they all look just the same."

That song was written about Daly City, the largest of the three places I would cover in 1977-78 as a reporter for the *Times* of San Mateo. Daly City had a population of something less than 100,000 and in contrast to nearby San Francisco, was a real working-class town. Its similar subdivisions that spread across the hillsides did indeed look like little boxes. Daly City boosters, trying to turn the stereotype around, called the rows of nearly identical house styles the city's "string of pearls."

The *Times* called about five months after we moved to Palo Alto and wanted to schedule an interview, based on my resume. I found out that I was one of two finalists and had high hopes going into the meeting.

But I was shy and nervous when the panel of editors interviewed me and worried that my height was a strike against me.

As usual, I took in the height of the men around the table (no women in those less-than-liberated times) and found only one taller than me. He was the son of the longtime publisher and we seemed to get along well.

I didn't get that job, but surprisingly, a few weeks later, the bureau chief called and offered me another that had also become vacant. I accepted with alacrity and was soon ensconced in a bureau where four reporters, a photographer, an assistant and the bureau chief worked in close quarters. My salary took a big jump: from $11,000 in Virginia to nearly $19,000 at the California paper, which was covered by a union, the Newspaper Guild.

I had to commute about 30 miles each way. Daly City's ocean proximity meant 300-plus days of fog each year; the inland location of Palo Alto, where we lived, gave it a climate that was sunny almost every day. Driving to work was akin to diving into a fog bank.

I was interested to see who beat me out for the original job. She was predictably short, with a cute, petite figure and much more self-confidence than I could muster. They always choose the shorter women, I thought with some bitterness.

Terry, who had a short haircut and a very young-looking face, remarked that at times her youthful appearance meant that some people didn't take her seriously. It was good for me to hear that; I'd never thought much about the downsides of short stature.

I liked her but felt way too competitive in her presence. I was accurate and a decent writer, but slow to get my stories finished. Terry could turn out stories faster without dithering about them, as I tended to do.

She and I saw a lot of each other because we both worked the odd 3-11 p.m. Monday shift. This allowed us to cover the night city council meetings on our beats without the Times having to pay us overtime. Like most newspapers, the owners found not-so-subtle ways to cut costs.

By the time I drove home those Monday nights, I'd written three or four stories (quantity was prized above all to fill the twice-a-week sections our bureau produced) and it was often well after midnight. The fog was usually thick and somewhat scary to navigate, but I managed.

On Tuesdays, my schedule again changed. I worked 1-10 p.m. so that I could cover the school district meetings, again without overtime. How I hated those meetings with their endless discussions by people who just wanted to hear themselves talk.

On Wednesdays through Fridays, I worked a more normal schedule from 9 a.m.-5 p.m. By this time, I had a hard time adjusting to the abrupt changes in schedule. I never did get used to that system, though I tried hard every week. I had no choice.

Len was having his own issues at Stanford. He spent practically all of his time keeping up with his demanding Business School schedule.

His only recreation was riding his bike the five miles to and from the campus each day.

You can't work this hard for two years, I told him more than once. He told me he had to, that he had no choice but to try to stay even with the mostly Ivy League grads.

I found friends, especially my friend Linda, another Stanford wife, who was always up for doing something adventurous. Together we explored wineries, local attractions and even camped with a few other friends on a nearby beach.

"We're having a lot more fun than our guys are," Linda said. I had to agree.

Linda was writing a textbook at home and worked at her own pace. By contrast, I was frantically busy covering the endless stream of meetings and other activities of a hectic newspaper beat.

The Daly City council meetings were much more riveting than the school board gabfests. At the time, the area had a lot of people of Italian descent and some were connected with the Mafia, or so we heard. Two older Italian men appeared at nearly every council meeting to complain about something.

The other two places on my beat were the town of Colma and the small city of Brisbane. I loved going to Brisbane because it was one of those places with a central, steep street and houses marched up a single hill. The people seemed friendly and it felt like a typical Bay area small town. Its lights looked beautiful at night, but unfortunately the city didn't produce any memorable stories.

Colma was different, a tiny town with a few thousand live residents and 90,000 who were deceased. It was known as the city of cemeteries because it was the place San Franciscans had started to bury their dead in the previous century.

Once I wrote about a Hell's Angels funeral where its local leader was buried alongside his Harley. The couple of dozen people who were attending gave me scorching looks so I kept my distance. It was before the time when I became bolder about confronting unpleasant – and possibly dangerous people.

By the time I'd worked at *The Times* for two years, I was sick of my job and of my boss, who never stood up for any of us in disagreements with management.

My supervisor, Will, was one of those hapless managers who couldn't do anything right.

Addicted to bargain-basement leisure suits, usually in a dreadful shade of green, he lived in a house where his do-it-yourself efforts were all too apparent. I don't know what his salary as a bureau chief was, but he seemed to struggle financially.

Once he had the whole bureau staff over for dinner where his wife served a thin soup containing a few cat hairs, several of us noticed. When one of guests said what a nice first course it was, he said tersely that it was the main course.

Len was finishing his MBA and interviewing for jobs, so we were considering possibilities, chief among them a Houston bank.

We wanted to go someplace different while we were still young enough for a new adventure. I desperately wanted to work for a big-city newspaper where I'd maybe escape the endless trivia of small-government meetings.

My last memorable California story was to interview a Daly City lawyer named Charles Garry. He was an old-style liberal who'd had an interesting career. He sang the praises of one client, a preacher named Jim Jones. I was skeptical. Jones sounded too charismatic and possibly dangerous.

My instincts were right. A few months later, Jones killed 900-plus followers with poisoned Kool-Aid in Guyana. Garry, who had come there to see his controversial client, made it to the airport and barely escaped with his life.

CHAPTER 16
LEARNING TO LOVE HOUSTON

As Len's graduation from Stanford Business School loomed in May 1978, we had big decisions to make.

Should we stay in the San Francisco Bay Area, where he had a fighting chance for a job at the giant computer company Hewlett-Packard? He'd worked there in an internship the summer before. However, I was weary of my newspaper job covering government and concerned that my chances of advancement at the paper were low. It was hard to move from the bureaus to the main newsroom because of heavy competition that skewed noticeably toward the male reporters. Somehow, it didn't feel right to stay.

We'd loved living in Palo Alto, but even after two years, it didn't feel like home. It was so pristine and seemingly perfect that I longed for messiness. We'd grown up in Virginia and North Carolina, and California was so far from our large, extended families. We'd go home once or twice a year and I felt I was missing a lot. Most people we met in California were charming, but it was daunting to get past the friendly, facile surface.

Should we return to Newport News or any of the other cities where we'd lived with our families in Virginia or North Carolina? My husband said that didn't feel quite right either, like taking a step back.

When Len got a job offer from First City National Bank of Houston, he told me he wanted to take it. Job offers weren't plentiful at the time and he was lucky to get a decent one.

Houston would take us halfway back to the East Coast, we reasoned, closer to our families and more like the places we knew. It would be exciting to spend a few years in a big city.

But we arrived in a July heat wave, with smoggy skies and traffic far worse than the Bay area. Our Toyota Corolla wasn't air conditioned and we used up $600, the last of our meager savings, to install cooling and put money down on an apartment.

I'd wanted imperfection, I had to keep reminding myself.

We spent all of the summer of 1978 adjusting to our new city. I called my mother one night from a phone booth near the apartment where the biggest roach I'd ever seen skittered too close to my sandaled feet. The apartment complex sheltered a rowdy bunch whose loud comings and goings beneath our windows mingled with sirens that disrupted our sleep. Our next-door neighbor said loudly to departing visitors, "Don't let your meat loaf." (Apparently a lame attempt to encourage his friends to have more sex.) On alcohol-fueled nights, pickup trucks regularly mowed down slender trees planted in the road's median. We vacillated between being amused and horrified.

I immediately went into job-hunting mode, personally visiting the editors of the two large competing papers, the *Houston Chronicle* and the *Houston Post*. Neither had job openings, though they seemed to like my clips from previous papers.

"Call me back," the *Chronicle* editor said. "I think something will come up in the next year."

Though that sounded less than ideal, I started calling the editor every couple of weeks. I also freelanced for the paper, writing stories about a suburban school district.

Meanwhile, as Len often reminded me, I needed a journalism gig that would augment our slender finances. In September 1978, I found a job as editor of a weekly paper in the suburban town of Katy. The small town was about twenty miles west of Houston and still had distinctive rice dryers from its history of rice farming.

I was disappointed working for a weekly after leaving a higher-paid daily's job, but I soon adjusted. The people who worked in the small office were Texas-nice and I made friends. I supervised a sports reporter who drove the back roads to games so she could smoke pot. (I didn't know that until I'd stopped working there.)

She was as tall as me, as was the paper's advertising director. Neither seemed bothered by their towering height and I marveled at their seeming nonchalance. Neither one was the least bit shy, as I still was.

As a reporter in a small town, I found that my height made me memorable, a definite plus. There were still plenty of "How tall are you?" comments but I was finding them less objectionable than usual.

Again, I covered local government and edited lots of neighborhood columns about weddings, new babies and social goings-on. Since this was a small operation, I also put together the layout of the paper and wrote the headlines.

The paper shared an office with a stationery shop on one side and I got used to its customers sidling up to my desk to talk about local politics. I sometimes wanted to tell them I had deadlines to meet, but the immutable customs of a small town couldn't be breached.

Nine months later, I got the job I'd been coveting with the *Houston Chronicle*, first covering Pasadena and a few other industrial towns east of Houston. The blue-collar refinery atmosphere of those areas was quite a change from the suburban/farming vibe of Katy. However, I found the refinery towns unique and enjoyable. I've found something to like about almost every place I've covered and have managed to find generous sources who'd help me find the real stories.

I didn't cover those cities more than a few months. My editor offered me a beat covering one of the largest school districts in the state. The Houston Independent School district had more than 230,000 students and several hundred schools scattered across the large central city area. I really began to learn Houston by visiting those schools.

I began seeing Houston through the eyes of a curious reporter. I drank it all in – the high life, the lowlifes and the lives in between. I went to rodeos, country clubs, barge christenings, dance halls, rooftop bars and icehouse dives.

In stories over the next few years, I would describe a seedy strip club I'd visited, the industrial areas around the Houston Ship Channel and hardscrabble areas on the East Side. The Houston I remember had both glitter and grime.

The newsroom was interesting, several connected buildings with an imposing front façade that gave the appearance of one unified building.

Inside it was reasonably modern with blue carpeting and a quiet atmosphere. The clacking of typewriters was giving way to the advent of computers.

Like most newsrooms, it had a few older men who could be charitably described as characters. In the era where reporters were still allowed to smoke in the newsroom, one older reporter would stub out his cigarettes on the carpeting all around his desk. I guessed no one had the nerve to tell him to stop.

One thing I loved about the newsroom was impromptu Friday get-togethers at a nearby bar in a historic building. My friends, mostly women in the Features Department, would gather there for relaxation and the gossip of the week. At the time, I was in my late twenties and early thirties, still young enough enjoy Friday night bar hopping. Len had his own friends who'd often go out on Friday afternoons.

Luckily for me, Texas had a bumper crop of tall women who seemed to enjoy their height, or at least accept it without angst. I remember meeting rich tall women at parties who dressed in the latest flamboyant fashion and even wore six-inch heels. Of course, as I told Len, they were usually fantastically curvy with lots of cleavage and plenty to spend on clothes. I felt dowdy when I was with such a glamorous crowd. Len's banking job meant that sometimes we were invited to fancy parties and I always agonized over what to wear.

I still have pungent memories about how Houston smelled (like burnt cork and the wet funk of almost-constant humidity) sounded (eighties hair-band rock music) and tasted (lots of great Mexican food.) I found neighborhoods I loved, restaurants I enjoyed, crazy traffic on sprawling freeways, but I didn't shy away from the city's underside.

The thing I enjoyed most about Houston was its realness. Houston feels genuine and like I'd half-hoped, messy. Though it has wonderful cultural offerings and other amenities, no one who lives there pretends that it's a perfect place. Its denizens accept it for what it is, and they don't seem to care what the world thinks about the city.

That's a huge contrast with some other places I've lived, where the movers and shakers fret incessantly about the city's image.

One of the other things I cherish is its people. I've never lived anywhere where people were more themselves – for good or ill. In Houston, I experienced friendliness, kindness and clear-eyed intelligence. I've also run across a few people who were as mean as snakes. Houstonians mostly don't hide their personalities or temperaments. Like the city itself, it's all there, every day, on parade. Messy.

CHAPTER 17
HIGHS, LOWS OF A NEWBORN

We'd been married six years and felt fairly secure in our Houston jobs when we started thinking about having a child. Our parents had been none too subtle about the subject, but we tried to ignore their questions. Now that we'd both turned 32, the issue was more immediate. But our feelings were mixed. How could we deal with two demanding careers and a baby? What would happen to my long-term plan to go to graduate school? At our ages, would it be hard to become pregnant?

It turned out that was not an issue. I got pregnant almost immediately. Still, I had nagging doubts. None of my married newspaper friends were pregnant or had children. But as my mostly problem-free pregnancy progressed, I became more attached to what was happening with my body. I enjoyed the attention, the feeling of having a larger purpose and even buying and wearing maternity clothes.

A rare bonus of being tall is that you can carry a child without looking too much like a blimp. I felt sorry later on for my short pregnant friends, one of whom said she felt, when she confronted the mirror, like she'd swallowed two basketballs.

When a male driver hit the rear of my car on the way to work, I felt immensely protective – and angry. Couldn't he see I was pregnant and especially vulnerable?

As B-day approached, I was looking forward to it. Finally, one day I woke up with what I self-diagnosed as contractions. I called my husband, who was already at work. He came rushing home.

"What are you doing?" he said, noticing me in the bathroom putting on makeup.

"I want to look good on this big day of my life," I said, applying pink lipstick.

At the hospital, labor progressed slowly until that evening. Jeffrey Stancill Norman was born on June 2, 1982. It's odd the things you remember. Because it was cold, I had put on white socks and one had a big hole in it.

Surprisingly, Jeff weighed only 5 pounds, 3 ounces, a fact that I took as a failure on my part. The doctor tried to allay my fears.

"Look how active he is," the physician said. "Don't worry about his weight."

But I did, of course. He wouldn't breast-feed, so I gave that up quickly, probably before I'd given it enough of a chance. When we took him home, he tipped the scales at a meager 4 pounds, 15 ounces.

At first everything was fine for us, the novice parents, but soon I succumbed to the postpartum blues. I cried when I uncovered his receiving blankets and looked at his spindly little legs, I cried when I boiled bottles, I cried especially when my husband went back to work. I was alone for the biggest responsibility I'd ever have.

My sister Diane in Virginia helped, but after our long visit with her, I still had to go it alone in Houston. I felt I was lacking the joy of having him in our lives. Luckily, I got professional help, which after a month or so put me back on an even keel.

I had wonderful friends at work, but when they occasionally came to visit on the weekends, it was though we were living on different planets. I handed Jeffrey to one male friend. He looked at the baby about thirty seconds and quickly passed him on to his wife.

In the next three years, things would change with my friends at the *Chronicle*. Most every couple I was close to, it seemed, was having a baby. But I suffered the loneliness of being the first in our set.

Len was a great help, but he generally didn't get home until about 7 p.m. By that time, I hadn't interacted with another human being all day. I didn't have a lot to say. MTV had just started its TV run and I watched a lot of it at night. Early mornings, when I was feeding Jeffrey, I'd put on bad cable movies.

We lived in one of those starter subdivisions in Houston that was bereft of trees and charm. It was the kind of place where everyone pulled out of their driveways by 7:30 to fight the dreadful traffic to work. It was hard watching everyone leave.

Except that one day, when I put Jeff in a stroller and walked down the block. I unexpectedly met another mom who was strolling her baby girl. She was an experienced mother who had two other daughters with her. She was attractive, tall with red hair and a ready smile. She sensed how lonely I was. She stopped to chat.

She quickly became my mentor and friend and she advised me on everything from sleep habits to diaper rash. During the four months I had for maternity leave, she continued to be a godsend. We kept up for years, but lost touch when she moved to Arizona. My attempts to find her have been unsuccessful because she has a common last name. Becky Miller, wherever you are, I wish you knew that you saved my sanity.

CHAPTER 18
A MECCA FOR JOURNALISTS

As a journalist, I had a strong work ethic, excellent editors and good ideas for stories. But nothing paid off as much as my membership in a professional organization called the Investigative Reporters and Editors.

The association, known as IRE, has more than 5,000 members across the country and some from around the world. Its influence is apparent at big newspapers and small ones, TV and radio stations and by freelance journalists. Its members pledge to help each other if asked and most members take that seriously.

I first became acquainted with IRE in 1988 when I went to one of its conferences, in San Antonio. I was hooked. There was an enthusiasm and dedication I had rarely seen, even in newsrooms. There was a great diversity of reporters and editors – tall, short, stocky, thin, white and minority, young and old. If there was any common denominator, it was a crowd where no one seemed to care about someone's looks or fashion (or lack of it.) There were jeans, shorts, Hawaiian shirts, corduroy jackets with elbow patches and flipflops. Not having to dress up was heavenly and gave me confidence as a tall woman. I bought IRE T-shirts and wore them faithfully for years.

Since then, I've attended more than twenty conferences in such places as Chicago, Phoenix, Miami, Kansas City, Portland and New Orleans. I've enjoyed getting to know the cities through the eyes of other reporters, late-night sessions at local bars and hotel-suite parties.

IRE has all kinds of traditions, like calling its members "the true believers" of journalism, only half in jest. Its emphasis on research is embodied in another venerable saying, "If your mother says she loves you, check it out."

I took my first class in computer-assisted reporting at a 1990 IRE week-long boot camp in Columbia, Missouri. IRE is located at the University of Missouri.

Since then, I've agonized over each new iteration of computer-assisted journalism. With IRE's help, I learned to combine and compare databases that have helped me with such stories as how often motorists are stopped for violations, how long the average divorce case lags in court and how many bars get inspected for violations.

I've met so many wonderful journalists over the years that I could staff a dozen newsrooms. In an environment where newspapers in particular are financially strapped, IRE does well because reporters realize they need those skills to stay marketable.

Journalism tends to be a lonely profession. Sometimes you feel like it's just you and your computer against the world. IRE eased that feeling for me, knowing that good colleagues would help if needed.

IRE keeps on hand about 3,000 tip sheets on how reporters did stories they presented at IRE conferences. I've contributed to that cache by speaking at the national conference several times. When my two novels were published, the association asked me to talk about the reporter and newsroom they portrayed.

I got so much out of IRE that I decided to run for its board to help with such things as policy and financial issues (and there were many of both.) I served on the board from 2003-2007.

One onerous duty of the board was fundraising. I came up with an idea that the organization adopted and still uses. I could see that reporters and editors from small newsrooms in particular had a hard time getting to IRE's national conference because of finances. The conference is the organization's primary training ground.

At the same time, I was looking for a way to honor my father's memory. He had died in 1995 after a lifelong career with small newspapers, and I wanted to do something to keep his good work alive. Why not set up a fellowship in his name that would send journalists from small newsrooms to the conference?

I started writing letters to all of his former newspaper friends and associates, as well as all of our relatives. I ended up collecting $32,000, enough to pay the conference expenses – from about $1,000 to $2,000 – for one journalist each summer. The money is supplemented by a larger fund.

I know that the mostly young recipients appreciate the fellowship from letters I get each year. The board thought the idea worked so well that a number of IRE members and other journalists have set up their own fellowships to honor living or deceased family members.

For me, it was one way I could begin to repay the organization central to my success as a journalist.

CHAPTER 19
FREEWHEELING LAWYERS AND CRIMINALS

During my first ten years at the *Houston Chronicle*, I covered a variety of different reporting beats and loved them all. (Well, except for transportation, which meant covering a lot of bus breakdowns in an aging transit fleet.) After that, I was promoted to the investigative reporting team, where I had plenty of memorable stories.

Long before that change, the news assignment that taught me the most was the federal courts beat. I liked the assignment so much that I kept it for four years.

It amounted to a free legal education. And oh, the fun I had covering fabulous cases, fascinating lawsuits and freewheeling prosecutors and defense lawyers.

I'd been covering the Houston school district for more than two years and was tired of school board meetings that often lasted from 9 a.m. to 8 or 9 p.m. Then there was the steady diet of internecine politics and the constant flow of "educationese," words that sounded good but meant little action.

I was thrilled when I got the federal courts beat. Unlike the criminal courts, federal courts were intellectual and varied. I wanted the drama of court trials but didn't want to cover a steady stream of murders, child abuse cases and horrific domestic violence. Our paper covered those types of criminal cases in state courts and a mixture of higher-level criminal and civil cases in federal courts, such as drug conspiracies and civil rights violations.

I started the beat around 1980 and stayed until 1984. In 1982, I left for four months for my lonely maternity leave. I was happy when I went back to work and resumed a journalist's job, even when hands-on mothering only in the mornings and nights left something to be desired.

Covering federal courts, I found my tallness to be mostly an asset. It helped me to project some authority (in situations where I often didn't have any) and certainly made me more memorable than some reporters. Of course, it worked against me, too. There were lots of short men (attorneys, federal agents, and especially unhappy defendants) who seemed uncomfortable when they went toe-to-toe with me in the halls and courtrooms. Some animosity was simply due to the fact that I was a nosy reporter doing my job.

The court beat also exacerbated the problem of dressing appropriately as a tall woman. Especially in the 1980s, I hadn't yet found a coherent style that worked for me, so I'd vacillate between polyester jewel-tone dresses and a modified cowgirl look of denim skirts, checked blouses and boots. Neither quite worked in covering courts. But at that time, we were scraping by, making payments for furniture and our first house. I didn't have the money to spend on the expensive suit ensembles the women lawyers wore.

I also had a hard time finding jeans that were long enough (as in most of my life) but that's another story.

In Houston, as in other big cities, a variety of reporters worked out of a designated pressroom in the federal building. The building was a drab 1960s multi-story structure with curious-looking square windows. The inside wasn't attractive either, but one advantage was a central bank of elevators. I could keep track of comings and goings.

Even better was the fact that our reporters' quarters were right across the hall from the grand jury room. Watching people file in and out gave me an advance look at who might be indicted.

The courts pressroom was a large rectangular office with five or six ancient metal desks, and chairs that never matched. My colleagues were the *Houston Post* reporter, my main rival, and two radio reporters, who filed versions of the same story hourly. When there was a big story, the TV reporters also showed up with their trucks and photographers. Usually they also carried stories that I'd written about the current case. They cribbed mercilessly from the print reporters' pieces because they only swooped in on the big stories.

I didn't really mind because I understood their job. They were sent out every day on several different stories and didn't have much time to develop sources or write big explanatory pieces.

Debbie, one blonde, attractive TV staffer I saw frequently, told me one busy news day that she loved reporting and would never want to be an anchor, even though it would give her more airtime and an office job.

"Reporting is the real thing, being out in the community and doing different stories every day," she explained on our way to a trial hearing.

The next time I saw her, she surprised me.

"Guess what?" She said excitedly. "I'm going to be a weekend anchor."

Other city beats, such as City Hall and Police had the same kind of setup as courts. The reporters would go directly to their respective pressrooms at buildings housing their beats and drop by the newsroom during the day, or late in the afternoon after they'd filed stories.

My newsroom was just two blocks away. I looked forward to the easy walk at lunchtime or day's end because I could catch up with my friends. My job offered an extraordinary amount of freedom that carried lots of responsibility. If the *Houston Post* beat us on a story, we usually had to answer for it. Our editors weren't often sympathetic.

One time I missed a big story. My editor growled that the early morning reporter had to scramble to catch up with "an abortion of a story." I wish I could remember what it was about. I'm sure I have purposefully blocked it from my mind.

My job consisted of covering major trials. Sometimes we decided the trial warranted gavel-to-gavel coverage. More often, we dipped in and out of courtrooms trying to get the crucial testimony without taking up the whole workday.

I also checked new lawsuits and judgments, sometimes hourly, because those were often worthy of stories as well.

And I did a lot of schmoozing with prosecutors, lawyers, secretaries and even judges. There were ten federal judges on the Houston bench so that translated into a lot of news. Sometimes I'd file four or five stories a day on the strange Texas Instruments machine that was a precursor to a computer. The judges all had different personalities with distinct work habits and writing styles.

I was eight months pregnant when I ran into a federal judge on the elevator and he looked straight at my larger-than-usual chest.

"Are you going to breast feed?" He said. "You know that's better for the baby."

Often trials would end late into the evening on Fridays, a hardship for anyone with children. Luckily my husband took the responsibility of showing up for end of the day-care shift in our neighborhood, though it was a detriment to his banking career.

Since I shared the pressroom with my competition, I used a lot of subterfuge to file an original story. Sometimes I'd go back to the newsroom to work or slip into someone's office in the building to make calls. Luckily, I got along well with all of my competitors. But we also understood that we were there to break stories.

Some of my most memorable stories involved a rogue ex-CIA agent who sold weaponry to Libya, a corrupt sheriff who ran an illegal speed trap north of Houston and a landmark case that tested whether Hispanic students should have bilingual education. (Both the rogue agent and corrupt sheriff got convicted and the judge decided in favor of bilingual education.)

Four years of covering federal courts added to both my competence and my confidence as a reporter. It also was a lot of fun. And it prepared me for the investigative reporting beat that came next.

CHAPTER 20
WAS I IN DANGER? I'LL NEVER KNOW

As an investigative reporter for ten years, five in Houston and five later on in Charlotte, I handled a lot of difficult stories and nasty people. But I never worried about my personal safety until I wrote stories about the corrupt leaders of a Texas community college.

The scandal provided story after story for nearly two years. In 1987, the *Chronicle* had promoted me to the paper's investigative team. The community college story was one of my first projects.

My height proved an advantage in this effort, because people, especially college critics, remembered me well enough to seek me out and offer tips. Also, I think my tallness made me appear stronger and less vulnerable to college leaders seemingly intent on harming me. I know that being six feet tall in this situation made me feel like I had an invisible shield of safety.

The story started with a phone call from a man named Ken, the Texas higher education commissioner and one of my secret sources. I'd covered him and his agency for about a year, and he and I had built a rapport based on trust and mutual respect. He often tipped me off to good stories.

He sounded worried that day as he talked about a strange place in Killeen that called itself by the grandiose name of the American Educational Complex. It had been run with iron control for years by a chancellor and president, two men hated and feared by the teachers and administrators they led.

"There's something about that place that just isn't right," the commissioner said. "We can't get to the bottom of it. But I'll bet you can."

The state board's hands were tied, he said, because most of the community college's money came from its local district.

"People in Killeen support the college because of the jobs it produces," Ken said. "The local board isn't going to do its duty by looking into problems."

His confidence was flattering, and I excitedly approached my editor about the call. A veteran journalist who nursed a deep vein of skepticism, Don wasn't thrilled by the idea of investigating a community college 200 miles west of Houston. But he agreed that I could do a Sunday piece about the place and we'd see what happened.

The chancellor and president of the AEC weren't happy either, but they agreed to see me. I'm sure that since I was interviewing people in Killeen, they'd become curious about what I was doing. I prepared diligently for the interview, dressed in my best professional-looking skirt and sweater and found myself sitting in a conference room across from them at the college.

The president and chancellor had brought in their public relations employees and cameras from the campus TV station. They shined bright lights in my face, an obvious intimidation tactic that didn't work. I'd been on TV in Houston at least half a dozen times to discuss stories.

"Why is a Houston reporter interested in our little community college?" Luis, the chancellor said. He was an overweight Hispanic man, about 60 years old, wearing a too-shiny suit. He had an air of menace mixed with faux friendliness that I took as a threat.

"I'm a reporter who covers higher education all over the state," I said, returning his fake smile. "Yours seems unusual and newsworthy."

His sidekick, the college president, a thin, balding man who wore a sour look and perpetual frown, didn't say much. But his dirty looks spoke volumes.

I plowed through my questions. The college taught a lot of soldiers. What was its relationship with nearby Fort Hood? Why had the college advertised in the local newspaper for well-trained military personnel? Was it involved with the CIA, as rumor had it? Why did the college call itself the American Educational Complex? Why didn't the two administrators associate with other community colleges?

After a few more questions that they refused to answer, the two men got up angrily and walked out. I followed them, continuing my questions until they disappeared into an office.

I got enough to write my Sunday story about the air of mystery that surrounded the ersatz Spanish-style campus, its ties with the military, reputed ties with the CIA and constant quest to win educational contracts. The college had started with Fort Hood and expanded its class offerings to other military bases, some foreign locations and even aboard ships. Among the normal community college courses, they taught some classified courses, including electronic warfare, which stressed clandestine communications.

The story, picked up and distributed statewide by the Associated Press, didn't go unnoticed. Sources began to call, fearful of being discovered and of putting me at risk.

About two months later, I started getting calls from a man who identified himself as a mid-level administrator. He said the president and chancellor were ruining the college. He gave me enough tips about financial shenanigans, and he called back often enough that I believed him.

Eventually, this man said he and a co-worker would like to meet me outside Killeen, in a shopping center near Austin. I think they wanted to check me out before giving me more information. I felt the same way about them. But I was hesitant. I arranged to call my editor by certain times before and after the meeting.

I arrived at the strip center destination and circled slowly before two men beckoned me from a car parked nearby. I said a silent prayer that I wouldn't be at risk when they asked me to get in the car with them.

They were both middle-aged men, who looked and seemed respectable and earnest about their enormous dislike of the top leaders of the college. We drove down on a country road and parked. They used the time to tell me what public records to request to show how the president and chancellor were using travel and other expenditures to skim unbelievable sums of money for themselves.

"You're in danger," one said. "We're in danger just by meeting you here."

They warned me that an instructor who'd tried to blow the whistle on the college a few years before had ended up drowned in the Houston Ship Channel. The same thing could happen to me, they said. I never could confirm whether the chancellor and president were involved in the teacher's death.

They brought me back to my car, we said our goodbyes and I breathed a sigh of relief. I'd taken a gamble, but it had paid off handsomely. Thereafter they became my best sources. I also got other phone calls and anonymous letters giving me tips and showing me how roundly employees hated their top bosses.

By this time, I was hooked on the story, convinced that a huge injustice was being done both to employees of the college and to taxpayers of that county and to Texas.

Using public records, I found that the two officials were giving themselves outlandish salaries and perks and using the contracts to hide their ill-gotten gains. One story showed how the chancellor had been reimbursed for $50,000 for taxicab fees supposedly spent over two months. I wrote story after story about their greed and corruption. But not much changed for more than a year. The local paper wrote stories about how I was harassing the college, using my name and calling me "the Wicked Witch of the East."

My sources continued to worry about my safety, insisting that I was being followed. I took precautions, checking into a different hotel every time I went to the campus and covering my tracks as much as I could. I checked out my car carefully, afraid that someone had tampered with it.

Family members worried about me too and urged me to wind up the investigation and get out. But my editors were giving me solid support, and I was determined to follow the story wherever it led.

One day I got a mysterious package in the mail. I opened it and had to laugh. It was a "wanted" poster featuring my picture, instructing anyone who saw me on campus to report it to the central office immediately. They'd copied the picture from one that had appeared in my newspaper. I laughed, but I was also horrified and found myself being even more cautious.

Finally, I wrote a story about how the two officials had bilked the state out of $10 million in a complicated pension fund scheme that involved double-dipping with state and federal money. That was too much for the higher education commission to ignore. The president and chancellor resigned the next day and a new reform administration was installed. The two officials were never charged with this complicated crime, and the state of Texas didn't try to penalize the college. I think officials realized that it would be a hard case to prove, and they were simply relieved that the old regime was gone.

I could breathe again, put my worry to rest and move on to the next story.

CHAPTER 21
A JOURNALIST'S NIGHTMARE

Are you stuck without a future? Do you lack the skills to get a good job? Are you ready to change your life in a big way right now? ... Don't miss the bus! Be there or be nowhere! *Flyer circulated by American Masonry Institute and Elkins Institute.*

While working at the *Chronicle*, I got a tip in 1989 for a potentially good investigative story involving scandal-ridden private schools.

Two shoddy trade schools had hired a raft of recruiters and turned them loose in New Orleans. They prowled the streets, persuading homeless men and women, drug addicts and other street people to get on a bus to Houston. The flyer they used was persuasive.

In Houston, the recruiters promised, they'd get free educations and wonderful places to live, cash money to pay expenses and a bus pass. They'd get training for such useful skills as data entry and they'd find jobs at such companies as Exxon.

What the two schools – American Masonry Institute and Elkins Institute – really wanted was for gullible men and women to sign federal loans, with the money going to the institutions. That would leave the homeless men and women owing thousands of dollars. If – when – they defaulted, U.S. taxpayers would pay.

I was outraged on behalf of the homeless people, who'd already had hard knocks in life. I resolved to tell their stories to the Chronicle's half-a-million readers.

Dennis, who'd lost his job as a cook, was one of the men on the buses. He told me he'd sold his meager possessions, signed federal loan documents for a $4,200 program and ended up penniless in Houston.

He and other program recipients told me they'd held an emotional meeting with the school's director, a man named Sayed, who finally agreed to give them $10 each. That might buy one Houston meal.

I talked to Sayed at length, hoping my height would be a little intimating to the much shorter man. I felt like I'd gotten his side of the story, which was basically that they were giving these students a chance to improve themselves.

Pretty soon, two agencies were investigating Elkins and AMI and barred the schools from the student loan program. Elkins closed shortly after. Sayed said he couldn't run it without student loans.

I was still doing follow-ups on the story when a manila envelope full of legal papers showed up at my desk.

Opening them, I found that I'd been sued for libel and defamation by Sayed. He also sued my paper.

I was crushed. I'd always prided myself on writing the truth and double- and triple-checking that my work was accurate. Don, my editor, was just as conscientious as I was.

I showed it to him, and he saw how upset I was. I was close to crying in our cubicle area at one end of the newsroom. Luckily, we were assigned to a quiet area with a lot of privacy.

Do you want to go home for the rest of the day? he asked.

No, just let me think about this for a few minutes, I said.

Ever sensitive to my feelings, he went back to a story he was editing. I just sat there and wondered whether I might have done differently. Nothing, I decided, regaining my composure.

The lawsuit accused me and my newspaper of destroying Elkins Institute. But the school's closure was preordained when it began signing up destitute students for government loans, then leaving them to forage at Houston food pantries when the students ran out of money. Some, like Dennis, complained to authorities.

About two weeks after Sayed filed the lawsuit against me, I met with the Chronicle's lawyer, a skilled attorney who had worked on a variety of cases for the paper.

We looked at the stories and discussed them at some length. He told me not to worry, that the truth was a complete defense. I had libeled no one.

I was comforted by his confidence and tried to be philosophical about the troubling event. I'd never been sued, though like most reporters, I'd been threatened with legal action many times.

I reminded myself why I was doing investigative stories – to help people like Dennis. The core of investigative reporting was almost as much a part of me as my height.

When he got to Houston, Dennis was placed in an apartment with two drug addicts. He left the place and got put in another apartment with two more addicts, who robbed him.

Broke and hungry, he used his complaint with the state as leverage to get back the $270 the school had cost him to sell his belongings for the move to Houston. He used some of that money to buy a bus ticket back to New Orleans.

A couple of months later, our company lawyer called and told me that Elkins' director had dropped the lawsuit against me and the paper. He didn't go into a lot of detail, but I suspect that with the state's actions, Sayed knew that the cards were stacked against him. If he lost the suit, which was almost guaranteed, he would have had to pay legal bills.

I had the satisfaction of knowing I'd stood up for people who needed it. And having anticipated an ugly trial, I was vastly relieved at the outcome.

CHAPTER 22
FRUSTRATING, EXPENSIVE TIMES

Around 1988, Len and I rather belatedly decided we'd try for a second child. Len's bank had been floundering, which had kept us from making that decision earlier, but the company seemed more secure for the moment.

I had also delayed a second pregnancy because I remembered the unpleasant experience I'd had with post-partum depression. With time, my fears had receded. We wanted a second child since we had enjoyed the first one so much.

Jeff was six, a good age to cope with a sibling without too much jealousy. At his age, he could be more of a help than a hindrance.

Although when I asked him if he wanted a brother or a sister, he said no, that he liked "my threed family."

The next day he came home from school and over dinner, he announced that he'd conducted "a survey" and found that none of his friends liked their brothers and sisters.

We both laughed and decided not to worry that he might be bereft without a sibling.

I was 39, as was Len, but our advanced ages didn't bother me. I had no trepidation about being able to become pregnant. After all, my mother had the last of her five children when she was nearly forty.

How wrong I was. Attempts to become pregnant lasted for four years and resulted in frustration, disappointment and financial hardship. I compared it to growing so fast and so tall as a young teenager and becoming awkward and accident-prone. My body, which was a source of satisfaction in that it thrived on hard work and unexpected challenges as a reporter, was betraying me again.

The attempts to become pregnant, oddly enough, coincided with a period of growth in my job. I'd joined the investigative team and was working on some of the best stories of my career. Perhaps the creativity in my work was sucking up all the fertility in my middle-aged body.

It seemed that everyone around me at the newspaper and elsewhere was pregnant or a new mother. I envied them the ease in which they got pregnant and gave birth.

When I'd gone for at least six months with no pregnancy, my doctor recommended endometrial surgery. I came through it just fine, but the only thing I had to show for it was a scar across my navel.

The tension in our personal lives was beginning to show. As we moved into more intrusive methods, my husband grew restive. He hated the process of going to the doctor and producing a sperm sample. I hated all of the tests, especially the monthly ultrasounds, which came up barren.

He wondered why we were doing this to ourselves when we had a great kid. He said maybe we should be content with what we had. But to me, pregnancy had become a quest. With each fruitless attempt, the stakes were higher.

Probably I would have felt better had I confided in friends. The only person who had the complete picture was my male supervisor, who needed to be told because of my frequent medical appointments. Again, he and his wife had no problems with producing children. Two and done.

I didn't share my quest with anyone else because I didn't want pity or questions every month about whether I was pregnant. It felt like a very private matter.

As we moved closer to in vitro fertilization, I believed that it was going to be my silver bullet. We did the daily shots in the hip (by that time, my husband had become a pro) and otherwise prepared for the big day. Alas, my small number of remaining eggs were basically of inferior quality and the doctors determined that I was closer to menopause than they had believed.

Menopause? I was only in my late thirties. That was something that happened to old women, not me. I was in my prime, well, not too far past it, anyway.

After that disappointing attempt, I was ready to quit – that is until I heard of a new program in San Antonio that used donor eggs. It involved getting on a list and traveling nearly 200 miles for the tests, physical and finally the surgery. I dreamed about my donor, a 32-year-old woman, and we decided to go for it.

My husband again was reluctant, especially because of all we'd already spent on fertility attempts. Some tests were covered but we'd still ended up in the hole about $10,000.

When my sojourn to San Antonio ended, I had nothing to show for it except the bills – another $7,000 or so. This time I'd definitely quit, and I did.

Except that I kept hoping against hope that I'd turn up pregnant one of those months after the treatment ended. I knew that it was highly unlikely and that I should retire those dreams. My husband and I told ourselves that we had one wonderful child, which many infertile couples would envy.

By this time, Jeff was ten and needed us more each year as he became active in sports and needed more monitoring with his academics.

What I learned, and it was a sad life lesson, is that no matter how hard you try and how fervently you wish for something, it may not happen. For a person used to going all out for what she wanted, and often getting it, infertility was a daunting realization. There would be other satisfactions – in my burgeoning career, stable home life and terrific son.

But the day you realize that you're never going to fulfill a lifelong dream is a bleak one indeed.

CHAPTER 23
FINDING HOME IN A NEW PLACE

I was sitting at my desk in the *Chronicle's* newsroom one morning when I got a call from a woman named Mary, then an editor for the *Charlotte (N.C.) Observer.*

"We're expanding our investigative team and wonder if you might be interested," she said. "Are you game to interview for it?"

I was interested because of our uncertain circumstances in Houston. Len's bank had been closed – for the second time in three years – and was purchased by its cross-town rival. My kind-hearted publisher had put in a good word for him, and he was now working for the new bank owner in a temporary job. We had no way of knowing if it would lead to something permanent.

Jeff was eleven, about to transition into middle school. My father in Virginia had just been diagnosed with bile duct cancer. It seemed like the stars had aligned for the move. North Carolina was a lot closer to my parents and siblings than Houston, could provide a permanent job for me and might lead to one for Len.

I'd met Mary, the investigative editor for the *Observer,* at the IRE convention and liked her. She was no-nonsense and obviously knew a lot about investigative work.

Mary was also tall, and I felt she might be a kindred spirit. I was impressed that women held most of the top jobs in the newsroom. Surely this was a good omen.

I interviewed and got a job offer. It should have been a fairly easy move, but I found, to my surprise, that leaving Houston was wrenching. The place I'd always seen as hot, humid and generally uninviting also held a lot of beloved friends and colleagues. Our neighborhood had beautiful trees, especially nice families from all over the world, and a great elementary school. What would the unknown hold for us?

"Do you think we should really do this?" I asked my husband one night as we enjoyed evening wine in our living room. At the last minute, I felt dubious and unsettled.

"Yeah, it's our chance to live in North Carolina," he said. "You know that I've always liked Charlotte."

We moved to the Queen City in 1993 when I was 44. Perhaps because of my age and stage in life, it was hard to make the lasting kind of friends I'd found in Houston. The reporters and editors for the *Observer* were more established, mostly had young children and weren't interested in having a Friday-night drink at a local watering hole, as my colleagues in Houston often did.

The uptown (most Charlotteans called it uptown instead of downtown) was attractive, with flowering plants and trees planted in the rights-of-way and plenty of new, mid-sized buildings. It was more manicured and much more visually appealing than any place I'd ever lived.

At one end of uptown sat the imposing newspaper headquarters. I thought the *Observer's* building was odd-looking, built in a 1960s architectural style known as Brutalism. It was square with four stories and long, narrow windows. Inside it had a central atrium with escalators, which always seemed to be out of order. The newsroom was dark with occasional slits of light escaping the narrow windows.

Most of the staff members seemed pleasant but reserved. I had to remind myself that it had taken me a while to make good friends at the *Chronicle*.

I liked the job. After being recruited for the newly expanded investigative team, I felt valued and useful. My tallness didn't matter; my competence to do the job did.

Mary, the woman who hired me, moved on to another job within a year, so I got a succession of three other supervisors. I had no complaints; Jim, Brian and Steve, who all held the investigative editor's job during the next few years, were skilled journalists, and all made my work better. I wasn't the easiest reporter to work with, always wanting to travel my own path and resentful of the layers of editing before a big project was published.

I spent five years on the investigative team with different colleagues who came and went for various reasons. I felt good about most of my projects. I wrote about workers compensation problems, the potential dangers of two nearby nuclear power stations and many deep-dive profiles of controversial Charlotteans, ranging from unprincipled lawyers to a strip clubs king. Sometimes state laws and local practices changed largely because of our stories.

My first project as an *Observer* reporter was a five-part series on food safety that we called "Watch What You Eat." I examined North Carolina's laws and practices and found plenty to worry about.

I looked at thousands of N.C. inspection records of restaurants, slaughterhouses and processing plants, finding that consumers weren't adequately protected from hazardous conditions.

Working on the series, which took about six months of reporting and writing before publication, convinced me that we'd done the right thing by moving to North Carolina. Since I'd lived in Chapel Hill for four years, I felt at home in the small towns and larger cities. If only I felt more at home in the newsroom.

Traveling around the state to food plants in obscure places made me happy by bringing back memories of college years. Most of the time I visited communities where I'd known someone at UNC.

I found it deeply interesting to visit pig slaughterhouses and chicken processing plants and didn't feel squeamish about seeing newly killed animals. Most of the larger plants were admirably clean and did a thorough sanitation process each night.

I couldn't say the same about some of the Charlotte restaurants I visited, finding that eateries could have roaches, dirty equipment and filthy bathrooms and still get satisfactory inspection grades. I made notes to myself on which restaurants to avoid.

One of my more startling findings was that the state and local governments didn't bother to inspect seafood markets or seafood sections of grocery stores, a major lapse in the wake of several seafood-related deaths.

I worried that my bosses would chastise me for spending so much time traveling and looking at records. To their credit, they realized that large-scale projects took months of work.

When the series came out in late January 1994, it drew interest and talk of reforms, especially in the area of seafood inspection. It later won a state award.

I was pleased with the attention, but more than that, I felt relieved. I'd worried about making a major change in my mid-forties, fearing that I was too old and inflexible to move to another newspaper. After the first project appeared, I felt that the transition was a success and I was on my way to finding a new home.

CHAPTER 24
`STARVING THE WIFE´

In 1994, I heard of a group of women who met regularly to exchange stories about the lack of progress of their divorces. I was intrigued and arranged to go to one of their meetings.

Most of the women were middle-class or formerly wealthy. They welcomed me warmly because I was the first *Observer* reporter to listen to their troubles. They said they were all victims of a legal strategy known as "starving the wife." The cruel practice referred to rich men's successful efforts to get divorce cases delayed indefinitely so desperate women would settle for pennies on the dollar.

This was despite a state equitable distribution law, called ED, that ordered courts to treat women as fairly as men when marital property is divided.

That didn't occur for Andrea, a 35-year-old Matthews woman. She and her young son shuttled between relatives and carried their belongings in her car for three years after her marriage broke up.

Andrea waited for court dates that never happened, lawyers that barely communicated and a case that never progressed. Finally, she gave up the fight for equitable distribution and accepted a small settlement that would give her and her six-year-old a home.

I noticed that the large house where I went to the women's meeting had leaks in the ceiling, and the hostess said she was financially struggling.

This was one of the clearest cases of injustice I had ever seen. I resolved to help these women any way I could.

I found that only about a fourth of the 34,000 North Carolina cases filed in 1994 sought a division of property. In my county, Mecklenburg, I was able to analyze slightly more than 200 of them.

In the great majority of divorce cases, there is little property to divide and spouses and their lawyers can make quick work of splitting the assets. The "starving" cases, in contrast, often involved many millions of dollars in assets, including such things as vacation homes and family-run businesses.

I had recently taken some journalism-based computer courses that would help me to quantify delays in pending cases and in cases that had been settled. I found that over half of the 200 cases I examined were still pending after two years. Settled cases were taking an average of two and one-half years.

In a few cases, some were still pending as much as nine years after they were filed. Judges often didn't even know how many equitable distribution cases they had in their courts. They were failing to monitor lawyers' delays because they didn't see a pattern that harmed spouses.

During the reporting on this story, I was really grateful for my height because I knew I'd have to interview some aggressive lawyers who were helping men to "starve" the women.

Sure enough, I met some lawyers for men who were stone-cold heartless, calling women names that were hurtful. One attorney in particular, called a woman named Aana Lisa "greedy" and said she had broken her marriage vows by committing lesbian sex acts. She said she hadn't. She commented that her husband's lawyer kept coming up with ways to cast doubt on her character to deny her the rightful share of the marital money.

He directed the husband to cut off Aana Lisa's household money and fire her from the family business. Two years later as the case dragged on, she said she had been forced to borrow $30,000 from her mother and had no cash to buy groceries.

The 56-year-old woman said her husband's lawyer ratcheted up the ill will between him and her – instead of guiding them to a settlement that would wrap up a traumatic period in their lives.

Finally, they reached a settlement that would give her close to half the assets she was entitled to – only because they were able to talk outside the scrutiny of the lawyers.

Being tall gave me the opportunity to stand eye-to-eye to interview that lawyer and others almost as heartless. Though I dreaded those interviews, I felt that my height helped me to hold my own.

The series generated numerous letters and phone calls and struck a nerve among local judges who were allowing the "starving" to happen. The chief judge vowed to cut the district's backlog of ED cases with more hearings and new policies that would discourage delays.

"We ought to be able to dispose of equitable distribution cases six to nine months after the entry of divorce," the judge said. "We need to do better and we're going to do whatever it takes."

And soon after the series ran, a legislative committee voted unanimously to endorse stiff sanctions that would encourage judges to punish divorcing spouses who would "delay" or "obstruct" court property-division cases.

There were other changes. Most divorcing spouses are now required to participate in dispute resolution sessions.

I'd never gotten such quick, emphatic results from a series. I was gratified by the local and state officials who were horrified by the "starving" situation and moved quickly to stop it. But I felt even better to know that I was changing lives for women who had been victims of a nasty, unconscionable policy.

CHAPTER 25

'SOLD ON SMOKING' A PROJECT FOCUSING ON TEENS AND TOBACCO

Early in my 15-year career at the *Observer*, I noticed some patterns about teenage tobacco use alarming enough to pursue an investigative project on teen smoking. It seemed like the right thing to look at in a tobacco state, especially since I saw a lot of young people with cigarettes. Smoking remains the largest cause of preventable death, responsible for about 400,000 fatalities a year.

I remembered beginning to smoke as a college student. It was very convenient; in our dorm basement at the University of North Carolina, near the washing machines and dryers, were vending machines full of cigarettes at the low cost of 40 cents a pack.

Luckily, though I smoked off and on until my early thirties, I didn't get addicted to it. I didn't smoke much, but I thought as a tall girl, it made me look sophisticated at parties. Actually, it was just the opposite. My friends assured me that I looked really goofy, like a teenager just learning to smoke.

In 1996, I started working on the project, not knowing that it would eventually take me to Tokyo and Beijing. I did know I had plenty of reporting to do in North Carolina.

Wherever I went, it seemed like I saw more youth smokers. Indeed, the statistics were grim. A poll showed that 30 percent of high schoolers in the state had smoked within the last month. The use of smokeless tobacco was common, too.

I talked to an anti-smoking advocate and asked her the best places to go to interview teen tobacco users. "Anywhere," she said, but noted she'd heard of one N.C. mountain community that had recently reported some startling statistics. In Robbinsville, in a rural area near the Fontana Dam, a survey showed that 70 percent of the high school students and about two-thirds of the junior high students smoked or had used tobacco recently. So that's where I went.

I found Jordy, a baby-faced 12-year-old who'd started dipping snuff when he was five.

"My dad dips, too," he said. "My mom and dad buy it for me, but I have to pay for it."

His parents acknowledged that was true but said they hoped Jordy would stop dipping.

Toward dark in Robbinsville, teens were hanging out outside a video games parlor smoking, dipping and chewing tobacco. Some were 12 or 13, some were 15 or 16, all too young to buy tobacco legally. But they didn't have any problem skirting the legal age of 18 at stores that sold tobacco. The teens were obviously bored, looking for something to do in a rather barren area.

In Yadkin County, not far from the tobacco city of Winston-Salem, I found two high schools that had built "smoke sheds," covered pavilions with cozy groups of benches. Between classes, students who'd gotten permits from home could go to the smoke sheds for a mid-morning tobacco break.

Some of the students said their parents didn't like their smoking, but they signed the permits anyway.

The students thought the smoke sheds were a good idea because even if it rained or snowed, they could enjoy their tobacco with the companionship of fellow smokers.

Why were such things allowed?

The legislature had weakened the laws aimed at keeping tobacco out of the hands of minors. There were technical difficulties prosecuting clerks or stores that sold to teens and the state didn't allow "stings" to catch illegal sales.

My bosses later sent me to China to cover an international anti-smoking conference and afterwards to Japan to cover an epidemic of teens smoking Marlboros there. The reporting was fascinating to me, and hopefully the reading public found the stories interesting. At the anti-tobacco conference, I went to ceremonies at the Great Hall of the People and listened to China's president and advocates from all over the world talk about the dangers of the addiction.

In Japan, I interviewed young teens who somehow thought Marlboros were the coolest cigarettes on the planet. Wonder where they'd picked up that message?

My project ended in 1998 when the tobacco industry and the U.S. government reached a multi-billion settlement that changed all the rules, including merchandising to minors. Now cigarettes are kept behind counters and clerks seem serious about checking identification of anyone who looks younger than 30, among other steps to cut down on youth smoking.

Our work and that of other reporters helped bring attention to the problems that exacerbated teen smoking. The groundbreaking tobacco settlement was forged by lawyers who had used the stories to point out the problems, some said.

Because of the massive tobacco settlement, many North Carolinians – including vulnerable teenagers – can breathe easier.

CHAPTER 26
MOVING FIVE TIMES IN CHARLOTTE

I tend to characterize my time in Charlotte by my work and the five places we've lived. Here are some thumbnail sketches of the lifestyle piece of the move, the places we've lived while we worked in this New South city.

We settled in a starter apartment for a few months in 1993. I signed up for this place near a fancy mall sight unseen. It was centrally located and well designed, with my husband and I on one side of the unit and Jeff on the other. The things I remember most are the ugly blue carpeting that didn't go with any of our furnishings and the thwack of the newspaper on our balcony each morning. Our time outside work was mainly spent looking for houses while we waited for a sale of our Houston house.

The less-than-ideal living situation didn't dampen our spirits, especially those of my husband. He quickly found a good job at Nations Bank (the predecessor to the Bank of America), a big relief after the temporary job he was doing in Houston.

"I was hanging on there by my fingernails," he said. "I felt so lucky to be moving to Charlotte and working for a big bank."

I said I liked my situation at the *Observer*, but I felt mixed about leaving the *Houston Chronicle*. Texas was a livelier place for an investigative reporter than North Carolina. Texas offered low-hanging fruit for stories, while I'd have to dig deeper in North Carolina.

As a permanent place to live, we found a neighborhood with two-story houses about ten miles from uptown Charlotte.

We lived in that house for nearly ten years, from 1993 to 2002. The house first seemed unpromising, with kicked-in doors, dated wallpaper and bad carpeting (again!) But we loved the subdivision, with its trees and organized social clubs. We'd never had a big house and this one had room to spare. Son Jeff quickly claimed the upstairs bonus room as his hangout.

Those years heralded a golden era raising our son. I was gratified that he grew tall, 6-foot-3, and felt like my height dividend was finally paying off.

I found him steadily more interesting as he grew into the teen years. He preferred skateboarding over any conventional sport and developed a coterie of like-minded friends. I felt that I'd missed a lot from his early years in Houston, because the demands of a news beat kept me working overtime. At the Observer, because I was assigned to long-term projects, I had more regular hours and more time with him.

I enjoyed his adolescent years especially because he had a goofy sense of humor and was always surprising me with his observations about life. He wasn't as dedicated to his studies as I would have liked, but managed decent (if not top grades) and good scores on standardized tests.

He had two serious girlfriends, so there was also the drama of dates, dances, proms and the inevitable breakups. His senior year he was a cheerleader who, as he put it, "threw girls up in the air." I just prayed he'd catch them on the way down.

He got into the three schools to which he had applied – the University of Virginia, N.C. State and Virginia Tech. It was evident that his heart belonged to Virginia Tech. Ever since he'd seen the beautiful stone buildings on the verdant campus, he was drawn to the place.

As high school graduation for the Class of 2000 loomed, I got progressively sadder as he got more excited. The day we took him to Virginia Tech was an all-time low for me. I couldn't stand the thought of going home to an empty house.

The house that once seemed ideal now seemed impossibly large.

"We're just rattling around in here," I told my husband. I said I hated to walk by his empty room and the bonus room with his half-size pool table and other special belongings. Urged by a next-door neighbor who was also moving, we put a down payment on a townhouse under construction in 2002.

We lived in an apartment complex for one year, from 2002-2003. Our townhouse near a major business and retail area surprisingly took a year to build in its new development, so we rented an apartment nearby. That turned out to be surprisingly fun. We'd walk to a boutique shopping area, for dinner or to see the snowflakes and holiday decorations.

I remember it as the year of the three cats. We moved in with two black cats, but one escaped early on. A friend talked us into replacing her with an adorable kitten. You can guess the rest of the story. The runaway cat returned and suddenly we had three black cats that either sprawled on the best seats in the house or followed us around incessantly. In a 900-square foot apartment, it seemed a little crowded, at least for the humans.

Finally, the new townhome we wanted was ready, but we only lived there for three years, 2003-2006.

The three-bedroom place was designed as the perfect empty-nester paradise. It had dramatic windows, good spaces and even a sizable landscaped back yard. It was impeccably turned out, thanks to a decorator friend. Yet it turned out to be a disappointment.

We'd hoped for a place with lots of new friends and community spirit, but on weekends the 29-unit project seemed devoid of life. We learned that many residents used their townhomes to connect with adult children and grandchildren in Charlotte during the week or as little as a few times a year. They often owned mountain or beach houses as well and spent weekends or weeks at those homes.

"Nobody's ever here," my husband said.

"I think we moved here about ten years too soon," I agreed.

It seemed like we were about the youngest couple there, not a recipe for close friendships.

After three years, we were restless to move again, this time finding a place about two miles from our workplaces in uptown.

We bought a 1927 bungalow on an older street abutting a much fancier neighborhood called Eastover. We fell in love with a one-story, brick house with a Craftsman design. The house has high ceilings, which suit my tallness just fine. It's not a fancy house but it feels homey. Every Friday night during the summer, there are neighborhood gatherings and we've gotten to know many of the residents.

We moved to the bungalow originally because it was near uptown. Now we no longer work in the center city, but we've had a ringside seat to the its growth.

In many ways, uptown has led the change from a sleepy city to a bustling metropolis. When we moved here in 1993, Charlotte seemed provincial. For instance, we wanted to go out on a Sunday night for our anniversary and couldn't find a decent restaurant that was open.

"Charlotte is so quiet," my then-young sister-in-law noticed on her first visit with her parents. This was after spending Saturday afternoon walking around uptown.

All that was to change during the more than two decades we've lived here. Charlotte is a boom town, with every available empty lot seemingly under construction. Is that a good thing?

I'm happy that it has more restaurants and other attractions, but sometimes I feel like an alien in a sea of young people. My tallness doesn't stick out as much as it used to, since many young women are growing taller. But people tend to ignore older, retired people, no matter if they're tall or short.

Do I want to spend the rest of my life invisible in a haven for young professionals? The jury's still out.

I still miss Houston, though when I return for visits, it seems like traffic is worse and the weather is hotter. But I was young then, with more fun-loving friends and opportunities to socialize. Perhaps the place where you were young and had the best times is the city you end up loving the best.

CHAPTER 27
A NEWSPAPER'S DOWNHILL SLIDE AND A PERSONAL SETBACK

My later years at the *Charlotte Observer* were mixed. On one hand, I felt that the original owner (Knight-Ridder) wanted quality journalism and was willing to pay to get it. I got superb training inside and beyond the newsroom, for instance. But in 2006, the *Observer* and its sister papers were sold to the McClatchy Corp., which was more interested in cutting costs and saving a buck or two wherever it could. In terms of great journalism, the sale was disastrous.

On Feb. 13, 2020, McClatchy filed for Chapter 11 bankruptcy and now is under the control of a hedge fund. That can only spell more trouble for the beleaguered chain.

We got positive feedback and won awards with stories from the *Observer's* investigative team, but I was beginning to feel restless. Five years after starting on the *Observer's* team (and another five in Houston), I convinced an editor to let me try part-time editing. For a couple of years, I filled in on weekends, assigning reporters to festivals, profiles and police activity, the latter which knows no difference between weekdays and weekends. It was a challenge for a shy person, but I thought perhaps my tallness lent more authority to my fledgling efforts. I wanted to make a different kind of contribution to the paper by working with people and helping them find good stories.

I moved into news fulltime as an editor of the crime and courts team. A large part of that time was spent on the indictment and trial of Ray Carruth, a prominent football player who was convicted in the murder of a girlfriend who was carrying his child. It was exciting and showed off the talents of two of the reporters I closely worked with.

I was assigned after a couple of years to the Features Department as an assistant features editor, a relief from a steady diet of straight news. I had one of the larger teams in the newsroom, which was challenging. The writers ran the gamut from gardening to food editor, from medical reporter to home editor. It was fun because it required me to learn (or at least become conversant) in so many areas. I edited stories ranging from how to cook Thanksgiving dinner to surviving the flu season to preparing a garden for spring planting. The reporters were all thorough professionals who had spent years covering their subject areas. I was an editor of that team for several years.

Mike, the top editor in Features made sure that I learned a lot and I quickly realized that my new assignment was very different from editing in news. For instance, more attention was paid to the quality of the writing and how the daily colorful sections looked in the paper. Creativity was at a premium and humor was encouraged.

I also began learning about the pitfalls of being an assigning editor. It was hard to please both supervisors and reporters on stories. Supervisors wanted more local stories to fill the daily sections, which meant preparing them faster. Not surprisingly, reporters often needed more time on stories to do a thorough job. The push-pull of competing interests was a tangle that was hard to resolve.

The next assignment, that of government editor, was problematic. There were major political shakeups in Raleigh, the state capital, that our staff of five was expected to excel in covering. Not only were we expected to report and write them; the goal, at first, was clearly to beat the rival *(Raleigh) News & Observer*. Sometimes, when our team was at its best, that happened, but often the newspaper in Raleigh got tips from being located in the capital city. When the rival got an important story first, I was usually the one who took the heat. I felt the need to explain and apologize. (Now the two papers, both owned by McClatchy, collaborate rather than compete; a necessity in the age of staff scarcity.)

Another tension centered on a disagreement over a reporter's evaluation. I don't really believe in negative performance reviews; I think they just discourage staff members from doing better. My bosses, however, felt that the reporter needed more criticism and tough feedback. This issue didn't get satisfactorily resolved, even though I relented and wrote a more nuanced evaluation.

One of my bosses suggested that I move from news to the business section to write a section-front column. The new assignment turned out to be an excellent experience. I reported and wrote a personal finance column for about eight months, centering on Charlotte area people with small businesses and topics of consumer interest. It was more fun than I initially expected, with stories on everything from new forms of cremation art to the costs of caring for sick pets.

Less than a year later, some openings came up and I was offered a chance to return to Features and work as the home editor. It was a hard choice, but I liked the prospect of tackling a subject I understood and enjoyed. I was glad that I had no one to supervise; I realized that I was a better individual performer than an editor, something I should have seen earlier. I delved into housing with alacrity.

About nine months after that move, in the spring of 2009, the newsroom faced more crises. The McClatchy Corp. had taken on two billion dollars in debt when it bought the *Observer* and the rest of Knight-Ridder's empire, which consisted of a couple of dozen large and small newspapers. Sadly, the sale of the once-profitable chain to McClatchy coincided with a downturn in the economy, which led to a steep decline in advertising and readership both at the *Observer* and at other of the company's acquisitions.

Layoffs at the *Observer* began in 2008. By April of 2009, there had already been three reductions in staff. The fourth, that spring, snared me and about thirty other colleagues who either left the paper or were forced out by greatly reduced work hours. (Since then, there have been many other layoffs. A newsroom that once had 235 employees now has less than 60.)

Worse, I learned about the staff reduction while we vacationed on a Caribbean cruise with friends. I called the office because I knew another layoff was to be announced and suspected it wouldn't be good news for me. When my editor said my job had been axed, the fun of the cruise abruptly ended. I felt shattered for the next few days and wondered if my journalism career could recover. But deep down, I realized that after

38 years in journalism, I was ready for something different. My biggest angst was how I would replace the income we'd come to rely on.

I could have found work with a smaller newspaper or regional magazine, but I felt that would be more of the same, albeit on a smaller scale. I realized that I'd been dissatisfied and bored for a while.

I needed to do something productive to keep busy and prove myself again. Back in Charlotte, I thought hard about it. One of my favorite subjects was housing; looking at sales, floor plans, trends and other parts of the residential business.

Within a month of the layoff, I was enrolled in the city's best real estate school in training to be a broker. I loved the classes and felt that I was headed toward something useful. The school took up a few months of my time and kept me from missing the *Observer*. Luckily my *Observer* friendships mostly stayed intact.

I passed the difficult state real estate exam on my first try, which restored some of my self-confidence. I felt that I'd landed on my feet, especially when a well-known brokerage took me on. (Since we were all independent contractors, we weren't hired and depended entirely on commissions.)

I worked all of two months for the excellent company, enough to go through their in-house training program and start finding my own way. A problem, I realized, was that many of my fellow brokers had been in the business for a couple of decades. They had long lists of contacts, and it was a fierce and competitive enterprise. Viewing the houses and getting the occasional call didn't contribute anything to my bottom line. I began to doubt seriously that real estate was a realistic path for me.

Then came a surprise that brought another giant change in life for Len and me.

CHAPTER 28
LONDON, AND A BOOK

We were astonished in 2009 when Len got an offer to go to London for two years. Bank of America had just bought Merrill Lynch and the Dutch official in charge of the overseas operation apparently chose Len for his calm behavior under fire.

At night, sitting in the living room with a glass of wine, we talked about it. My husband was hesitant to consider the offer seriously, to which I replied, "What? Are you crazy? You'd be foolish not to take it."

I was ecstatic over the thought of living in London, one of my favorite cities, and couldn't understand why he would worry.

We started making preparations for the move, which I considered a grand adventure. Len still acted dubious about it but came around. Since we were considered expatriates, we got some perks, including help renting our Charlotte house, storing some belongings and moving others. We took a reconnaissance trip to London to look for apartments and found that what seemed to be a generous allowance didn't go quite as far as we thought. But after much searching, we ended up with a nice three-bedroom unit in Chelsea, one of the fashionable close-in areas. It turned out that Chelsea, formerly an artists' colony, was now a haven for rich Russians, other Europeans and Far Easterners. They wanted to park their money in a safe place, but rarely stayed in Chelsea more than a few weeks a year. At night, our condo building looked positively barren.

We were lucky, however, to become friends with the next-door English couple, Von and Barry, who turned out to be everything good neighbors should be. Barry taught us a lot about England and Von was funny and generous with her time. We still keep up with them and visit back and forth.

It's hard to describe what those first six months were like for me. Len worked at least ten hours a day and I was left to amuse myself, often alone. I walked a lot, swam in the municipal pool, shopped on the Kings Road of Chelsea and went to museums, often by myself.

I became a member of the Kensington-Chelsea Women's Club and the American Women's Club, which perked up my social life. The AWC particularly had activities almost every day, including bridge, Mah Jongg, day excursions, trips, lunches, dinners and weekly trips to the pub. I took advantage of much of it.

But I was still restless, a little lonely and thought increasingly about my pent-up desire, writing a novel based on my experiences as a reporter in Texas. I had some ready-made stories, mostly difficult reporting situations I had overcome. I thought I could use those experiences to my advantage. I wanted to create a reporter heroine who'd be a little like me, but prettier, younger and more outgoing.

Most of all, I wanted to create a tall protagonist, one who stands 6 feet but is proud of her height. She is beautiful, with long dark hair, elegant legs and an intuitive mind for investigative reporting. She has two handsome men vying for her favors who find her tallness attractive. People in general flock to her because her height and her personality are intriguing.

I wanted to use my height to my fictional advantage, to show that tall women could be just as alluring as short females, even more so.

I started writing and tried to devote a few hours a day to my book project. I loved Annie Price, my protagonist. She was a counterpoint to all the tall jokes and inane comments I'd suffered over the years.

But I found that to my chagrin that I was getting hopelessly lost. My loose plot was sending me down rabbit holes and other detours I knew were sucking the life out of the book.

Then a friend visiting London recommended Ian, a writers' coach, a British man who lived in Minneapolis. I contacted him and he was more than happy to work with me, especially when it involved trips to London, his hometown. He happened to be there at a book fair so we could meet in person. Luckily, we clicked and began a fruitful professional relationship.

He showed me how to draw diagrams about what might happen and talked about chapters I'd written that I should consider ditching. He told me I had too many characters and an overload of plot lines. Like a sculptor, I should consider carving away the excess and work with what remained.

The centerpiece of the novel became Annie Price's attempts to solve several murders behind a modern-day secessionist plot to take over Texas. There's a secessionist candidate for governor, a decent guy who unfortunately has a nest of vipers supporting him who manipulate and kill to achieve their fascist dreams.

Some of the plot was based on my experiences with the corrupt community college in Texas and its ruthless leaders. There's also a lot of action and scene setting in West Texas, an area I've always loved.

What gives the novel an additional plot line is the gubernatorial candidate's interest in Annie and her fascination with him. Also, there's another politically powerful boyfriend lurking in the background and an amoral reporter with sexual designs on Annie.

When the book came out, some readers felt that Annie was promiscuous because she had three men interested in her, but I reveled in the tall girl's attractiveness to men.

For a year or so, I'd write a chapter or two, and Skype with Ian about it. It was a good way to work and I felt I was getting good critiques. We didn't always agree, but I'd see there might be another way to go.

Len was able to get an assignment for a third year in London, so I tried to make the most of the time to write and to travel. We took more trips, including Egyptian and Greek cruises and a sweltering visit to Morocco. We saw most of France and Italy and much of England. It was an exciting time.

But my book was always at the forefront and I had a decent draft by the time we left London in late 2012. I was eager to find a publisher and spent a lot of time perusing a copy of The Writers Market, the big book listing agents and publishers. After sending out about 100 emails to prospective agents and publishers, I finally found a small publisher in

Texas, Black Rose Writing, which was willing to take a chance on *Saving Texas*, as I called the novel.

After editing and finishing work, my book was published in October 2013. Then came the unnerving task of publicizing it. I worked hard to set up bookstore readings, library events and book club appearances. I was proud whenever there was a flurry of sales (which I could check on Amazon) and disappointed whenever there was a dry week. The book mostly got good reviews in statewide papers and still occasionally sells a few copies.

One of the most rewarding experiences of my life was seeing my fictional tall girl triumph. The protagonist I'd invented seemed almost real to me, was memorably beautiful and lacked the debilitating shyness that marred my social life.

I felt my Annie was everything I wasn't. Creating her was the peak experience of my professional life.

CHAPTER 29
GRAD SCHOOL AT LAST

When we returned from our three-year stay in London, I decided to apply to a master's program in creative writing.

I first applied to the master's program at Queens University, fairly confident about my chances, given the fact that I'd written (in my eyes, at least) a decent book-length manuscript. I was disappointed with the subsequent rejection. They never bothered to formally notify me, so I had to keep calling to find out their decision. Not classy, Queens.

In fact, I was so angry I was determined to get into a master's program somewhere. I noticed that the magazine Poets & Writers had a full-page ad from the University of Tampa, saying the school was taking late applications. I called, asked some questions and prepared a quick application. I was accepted for the upcoming summer term.

The university, like all I was considering, was a low-residency program. That meant I'd go to Tampa in January and June for ten days each of instruction and intensive work. I'd choose or be assigned a mentor who'd critique my work on a monthly basis. I had already decided to write a sequel to *Saving Texas*.

(The university recently announced it would end its low-residency MFA program because of low enrollment and the proliferation of other programs that are chasing too few students.)

I had two tasks ahead, one of which was the continuing work of publicizing the book. I'd always wanted to publish a novel and I'd long felt almost ashamed that I didn't have a master's degree.

It was a busy time, but by the time I arrived in Tampa, I felt that I'd laid decent groundwork for the novel and was ready to pursue the graduate degree. I was ecstatic to be in school again after 40-plus years. Just being in a large lecture hall with 90-plus students was invigorating.

Proving myself was a challenge. I was surprised that I felt as shy as a teenager. As usual, my height was part of it, but making an impact in a new environment also was a huge challenge. I was one of the older persons in the program, though there were a few others in their sixties. Being around cute young (and short) women wasn't exactly a confidence-builder. Of course, some of the teacher-mentors were noticeably younger.

One mentor, a striking African American woman a little taller than me, particularly drew my attention. Not only did she exhibit an abundance of confidence, she often wore six-inch heels. I almost never wore heels. If I did, they were usually of the two-inch variety. She is a prolific poet and later became head of the program.

Then I read a story she'd written in the Tampa weekly arts newspaper about her loneliness as a single woman. She had a local bar where she hung out, hoping to meet unattached men. I was surprised. Because she was such an icon, I'd assumed she had everything she wanted. But again, it seemed to show that particularly tall women had a harder time finding dates than their shorter sisters.

My height also gave me the usual trouble socializing at bars and parties. I've always felt I had to bend down to hear what the shorter person was saying. That is still a problem for me in the shorter world, especially since my hearing isn't quite as good as it used to be.

I found a wonderful group of women to eat lunches and dinners with, but few wanted to have a glass of wine or a beer after the program for the evening. (Every night a writer or two read from their work for us.) A few times I went to the popular watering holes with someone, but I felt out of place with the mostly male mentors who hung out until 1 or 2 a.m.

The first residency was a revelation. I loved the two-hour workshops where our group of six writers critiqued each other's work and we got to read and hear criticism of our own efforts. The sessions held in the big auditorium were also interesting, as the school brought in established writers to lecture on craft subjects, including such literary lights as the late Denis Johnson, Roxane Gay and Leslie Jamison.

I couldn't believe how much I gained by this experience. Everything about it seemed magical. We stayed at a hotel on the Hillsborough River where I could open the blinds and see boaters sculling every morning. We'd walk over a scenic bridge to the University of Tampa for 9 a.m. sessions. The university has a central icon – an administration building that once was a turn-of-the century hotel. It has minarets that are visible for several miles. I was fascinated by those exotic-looking structures on top of the building, especially the way they looked lighted at night. I must have taken a dozen pictures of them, marveling at my luck in being in such an interesting place.

About two-thirds of the students attending were working on novels. The remainder was mostly poetry students and fewer than a dozen in the creative nonfiction section.

The subsequent residencies (there were three in which we pursued our projects and another when we graduated) just got better as I learned which mentors were right for me. Tony and Stefan improved my second book-in-progress tremendously and encouraged me about the thesis project we all had to write. They still offered unvarnished criticism to improve the new manuscript's believability, which I appreciated. They didn't mince words about shortcomings, but they were kind and sensitive about it.

One of the most difficult parts of grad school was the requirement to write a lengthy term paper. I suggested one comparing the language used in J.D. Salinger's *The Catcher in the Rye* and David Mitchell's *Black Swan Green*. Since I'd done decently on papers in college, I thought I'd breeze through it with little trouble. Wrong! My mentor urging me to do more research and he was right. It was a lesson in avoiding overconfidence.

I got through most of my new novel in a skeletal form, which I knew would need considerable revision after the program ended. That was okay – I thought it was deeper than the previous book and I could visualize what it could be.

On a hot day in June 2015 (Is there any other kind in Tampa, Fla.?) about 25 of us (the class that had started in June 2013) walked across the stage in caps and gowns. All of my mentors were there to wish me luck. I was unexpectedly moved by the ceremony.

I was on my way to finishing the second book and waited to see what the future would bring next.

CHAPTER 30
'WINNING TEXAS,' LOOKING AHEAD

My mood vacillated between joy and sadness when I finished my creative writing degree in June 2015. I took some R&R, but that fall I got back to revising the sequel that I was calling *Winning Texas*. My mentors had assured me that it was far superior to the first book (the ones who bothered to read the first book) but I had my doubts.

Unlike the first book, which utilized many of my reporting experiences, this one was a product entirely of my imagination. I kept adding new characters and subplots, with the result that murderous action tilts to the second half of the book. In *Saving Texas*, I tried to have surprises (and killings, of course) spread evenly throughout the book.

Winning Texas opens with some decent action. The floating body of a woman is discovered in the Houston Ship Channel. Annie, my tall, slender and smart protagonist, goes out to investigate. She's now an editor and she's filling in for her police reporter because he's on assignment. She runs into her favorite police detective and they lay the groundwork for probing the mystery. Their formerly professional relationship also eventually becomes a romantic one, with disastrous results.

Annie gets caught up in a plot where the violent and disgraced Texas secessionists are regrouping to fight a rival group, peaceful people who want to create a tourist-friendly enclave called German Texas. Annie's forays into the area uncover another secret so illegal and lucrative that her life is threatened. On a visit to a hidden ranch, she gets shot by the owner and barely escapes with her life. In another plot twist, she's thrust into Houston's sleazy world of topless dancing to help a former boyfriend looking for his daughter.

As you can probably tell, this is a complicated plot effort aided and abetted by my mentor, who didn't hesitate to say when he thought the action was pedestrian. He helped to make the novel as good as it could be.

I feel that the second book plays to my strengths as a writer. I love suspense and surprises and made sure the second half of the book contained three big ones. Two involve seemingly moral characters whose weaknesses and corrupt deeds are exposed with Annie's help. The third surprise involves a twist on babies for sale.

Like most writers, I love, and I hate writing. I enjoy figuring out what the book needs – more action, for instance, or romance or atmosphere. But I dread sitting at a desk and spending hours at the computer making those scenes come alive. I think I must have a touch of Attention Deficit Hyperactivity Disorder. On the other hand, I love having written if I had something incisive to say.

When Black Rose Writing, my publisher, found that I was almost finished with a second book, the company's owner, Reagan Rothe, promptly offered a contract to buy and publish it. I was flattered and decided to continue with the San Antonio-based company. It had treated me well and seemed thrilled with my first book's healthy sales of paperbacks and e-books. Rothe knew that I was a dedicated publicist, setting up readings and appearances in Houston and all over North Carolina. I did it myself at the start, but later acquired the services of a publicist for a few months.

As often happens, it was harder to create buzz for my second book and appearances and sales were underwhelming. Despite that, I did the best I could, with an especially nice event at a bookstore in Houston. However, after writing two novels, I felt I was at least temporarily drained of ideas and energy for a third long work of fiction.

But I couldn't get Annie, my six feet tall protagonist off my mind. I regarded her as a better version of me – young, beautiful and confident while I struggled, especially with self-esteem. I wanted to chronicle my own life – the good and the bad – about being a tall woman.

So that's what I've done.

CHAPTER 31
WERE THESE MY PEOPLE?

Many years ago, a young lady wondered why
Legs bumped the table – and that's not all
Beds did not fit, some people were shy:
There wasn't a club for anyone tall.

She formed a group for anyone able
To bump their knees and legs under the table.

Chorus: Tall Clubs International:
A common bond by friends shared by all
Tall Clubs International: Heads above the crowd, standin' tall

From Founder of the Tall, Tom King, 1990

It started with a very tall young woman. Kae Sumner, a 6-foot-3 artist with Walt Disney Studios, wrote a wry, self-deprecating piece in 1938 for the Los Angeles Times about life as a tall, single female. It created a local sensation and Sumner yielded to pressure to start the first tall social club in the United States, the California Tip Toppers. That organization didn't take long to morph into a network called Tall Clubs International, with groups scattered across the nation. Sumner married a tall man she met in the social club and became an enduring touchstone for tall women everywhere.

That's how I came to Portland, Oregon, bracing myself to meet the women and men gathered for the TCI convention. I'd read about it on the Internet and eagerly signed up for the 2017 annual meeting. I'd probably missed hearing about tall clubs because the South had none. Most were centered in the western states and the Northeast.

At six feet, I was barely tall enough to qualify for the meeting. Convention rules specified minimum heights for participants: 5-foot-10 for a woman, 6-foot-2 for a man. My husband, at 5-foot-10, was ineligible to attend and furthermore, had no interest in participating in a group that would regard him as a pipsqueak.

I looked in the mirror in my bargain-priced room at the Red Lion Inn and wondered why I'd flown across the country to gather with 110 strangers at a convention where we shared one common denominator: our height.

Suddenly, I felt as exposed as a telephone pole. Did I actually have to talk to strangers for four days? Did I really need to do this to understand today's tall life?

Would I feel at ease among some of the tallest people I'd ever seen? Yes and no. I met dozens of nice people, but the convention itself felt like a time warp, a sweet throwback to the 1970s.

Most of the women at the convention stood 6 feet 1 inches or taller, and the men on average seemed to hover around 6 feet 5 inches, nothing you wouldn't routinely encounter on a football field. There were of course taller men, including a man named Dave who stood close to 7 feet. What seemed more noticeable, on first meeting, were people of advanced age with heavy physiques, particularly among the single women.

Most of the men and women attending the convention appeared to be between 50 to 70 years old. A few appeared in frail health and it wasn't uncommon to see someone using a wheelchair or a cane.

Megan Lukens, a convention organizer and the TCI's web master, said many members joined local tall groups in the late 1970s and 1980s. Men and women enjoyed the camaraderie – and often, romance – they found at national conventions and regional meetings. They stuck with the organization as an integral part of their social lives, finding dates, mates and friends across the country.

"I've heard it was pretty rowdy in the 1970s," she said. "It's different now. There are so many ways for tall singles to meet on the Internet." Women attending the convention outnumbered men about 3-1.

Lukens, a striking, outgoing woman with long, grayish blonde hair and a penchant for purple outfits, said she joined the Portland Skyliners Club in the 1980s. At 6-foot-4, she fit right in. It didn't take her long to find friends, and even a short-lived stalker, before meeting David Lukens, the man she married, at a tall club New Year's party. Like many taller women in the 1960s and 1970s, she found it a challenge to develop a social life as a teenager and young adult.

"Young tall women need to know that there's a light at the end of the tunnel."

"Now there are second-generation and third-generation tall club members," she said. "But all of the remaining clubs struggle to attract new members, especially young people."

Other club members echoed that thought. A man in his 60s from Atlanta said he's in at least three meet-up groups, mostly for basketball and dancing activities. "Still, the conventions are a good way to explore a new city and a good, cost-effective vacation," he said.

Lukens said she hopes the tall clubs will endure, but the downturn in members is troubling. However, she said, there's still an obvious attraction. "It's a relief to go to Tall Club activities and not have people staring up at you."

That evening featured one of the odder TCI traditions: The Miss Tall International pageant.

Lukens had told me about her experience with the national pageant when she was Miss Tall Portland 1987. She was one of 19 contestants that year in a contest that included a swimsuit round.

"Participation in the pageant has steadily dropped, in part because some of the younger women feel it's anti-feminist," she said.

Not so Valerie Ahrens of Chicago, a zaftig blonde who was crowned Miss TCI International in 2014. A coterie of tall members supported her successful candidacy. Ahrens, an attractive woman about 30 years younger than the average convention attendee, said the title has given her continuing cache.

"I really wanted it," she said. "My boyfriend still introduces me as a beauty pageant winner."

The Portland pageant consisted of just two contestants, an older blonde woman from Portland and a young brunette singer from Vancouver, Canada. I wondered why the convention organizers had persisted with the contest with just two women vying for the title. It seemed particularly awkward, but I concluded it was too much a part of TCI tradition to scrap.

Despite the low participation, there was no shortage of beauty pageant atmosphere. The ballroom was festively decorated with paper flowers and the announcer included a local, Bert Parks-style host. The two woman performed talent acts, strutted on stage and answered several questions. There was no swimsuit competition. I didn't think I'd find it particularly interesting, but it turned out to be fascinating.

All of the "retired queens" were recognized, including Valerie Ahrens in a stunning red dress. Eventually the judges selected Lindsay May of Vancouver as winner. I felt some chagrin for the other woman, who was an attractive blonde but considerably older than the 20-something choice. It sounded like she'd overcome a lot of challenges in her life, including a 100-pounds-plus weight loss.

The men at the convention gloried in their tallness. They said they enjoyed standing out in a crowd and believed that being tall brought power and popularity.

"I absolutely love being tall," David Lukens of Portland said. "The only downside is buying clothes and fitting into small spaces, such as airline seats."

The women, however, were much more equivocal in their answers, remembering being bullied in middle school and high school, especially by being called humiliating nicknames, such as Olive Oyl (Popeye's unattractive girlfriend.)

Some replies were wistful, such as one by Sonia Conisarev of Austin, Tx.

"One time I walked into a restaurant ladies' room and saw a beautiful girl who was tall and wore higher heels.

"The girl said, 'I'm 6-foot-1 and I love wearing heels. I'm about 6-foot-5 in them," Coniserev, who is 6 feet, recalled. "I was wearing two-inch heels. At that moment, I wanted to be her."

A middle-aged, slightly overweight woman (6-foot-4) sat by herself on a sofa during a late-night happy hour. Resignedly, she said she found a sameness about the conventions. Men flocked to the younger, novice, 6-feet convention-goers while the older, taller women were mostly ignored.

The next day, I left the convention with a sense that tall clubs were mostly a product of bygone days, when tall women were fewer and far between and struggled to meet men. Long before Tinder and other social media apps and before Title IX had made it more desirable to be tall, women of stature needed a helping hand.

I felt a kinship with the women I'd met. But I was luckier. When I was a young newspaper reporter, I had chances to meet men in a more normal setting. The tall conventions favored men, who were almost always outnumbered by women members. I had the feeling that many men had used the meetings as sexual hunting grounds, while the women mostly wanted to snag a husband. And as usual, the deck was stacked. The taller, older women took a back seat to the shorter, younger females, just like in real life.

CHAPTER 32
A GREAT TIME TO BE TALL

Marrying Len Norman, the love of my life, raising our son; finding a satisfying career as a journalist; and writing two novels have been high points in my life. My height seemed to color all of those parts.

As I grew into a reasonably confident woman from a shy teenager, American society in the 1970s was beginning to accept that women of different sizes, shapes, and talents all have value, from the tallest to the shortest females around.

But I've read academic papers of the 1950s and 1960s that emphasized how much men preferred shorter women, often as petite as 5-foot-2, to date and marry.

Is it any wonder that some parents of tall girls, especially in Europe and Australia, went to doctors who prescribed growth-stunting hormones from the 1960s and even into the 1990s? The practice mostly stopped when the women treated began having troubles with fertility and other female problems.

Or the highly publicized but rare case of Ingrid Westman in 1964, when she and her parents begged a doctor to cut into and shorten her thighs to lose a couple of inches from her 6-foot-1½ frame? After the operation, *Parade* magazine assured its readers, she was happy because she was more popular with men.

The passage of Title IX in 1972, which banned discrimination in female sports to those of males, made the country take notice of tall women who excelled at basketball, swimming and other sports.

The legislation helped Jamie Brown, now 42, of Charlotte, who won a basketball scholarship to Davidson College. She grew up to value her height.

"Height has helped me tremendously with confidence," said Jamie, 6-foot-1, who operates four restaurants with her husband. "You put a tall woman in a suit and she looks the part of an executive. You feel like you could apply for any job and get it."

I had arranged to meet Jamie at a local café and she greeted me with warmth. A slender woman with long dark-blonde hair, she wore jeans and three-inch wedge booties. I admired her sense of style as well as her friendly personality.

Does she ever have awkward moments as a tall woman?

"I don't want other people to feel small or slight," she said. "When I'm speaking with shorter women, I have this lean-back pose to get eye-to-eye."

A tall, younger woman who has benefited by the changing opportunities for females is Charlotte's Audrey Burri, 18, 5-foot-11.

Burri, who has a promising career in the world of modeling, this year won a rowing scholarship to Notre Dame. She has also excelled in a number of beauty pageants.

"I think that my height has added to my self-confidence," she said. "Being tall for some reason makes people view me as older. This encouraged me to buy into a more mature attitude at an early age."

These women and millions of others have come of age when it's great to be tall.

As a young woman, I could tell that the world was changing in favor of accepting women's differences in appearance, but my worry about my height was so engrained that it took me longer to appreciate being 6 feet tall.

As I became a journalist, a career that gave me much pleasure, I would vacillate about whether my height was good or bad. Sometimes, especially when I had to interview recalcitrant subjects, being tall was a distinct advantage.

Other times, I blamed my tallness for a variety of unrelated situations – slowness in making friends and other difficulties ranging from getting pregnant to getting good jobs. I've known in my heart that there's little connection in my height to most of life's opportunities and disappointments, but at my lowest points of self-esteem, I tended to find fault with my tallness.

But most of the time, when I'm all dressed up and I look into the appreciative eyes of my husband, I glory in my height.

NOTES

My story includes the best of my memories about my life, and research into female issues including leg surgery, hormone treatment and dating trends. In one chapter, a pseudonym is used for a friend whose life situation has changed drastically. In every other situation, the first names used are correct. First names are used because the subjects may not remember the incident chronicled in the book.

Here are research sources sprinkled through the book:

1. Lloyd Shearer, "How to Shorten Too-Tall Girls," *Parade* magazine, August 23, 1964.
2. Alison Venn with six other researchers, "Oestrogen Treatment to Reduce the Adult Height of Tall Girls," *Lancet*, October 23-29, 2004.
3. Roger Dobson, "Why is the Woman on the Left Considered Superior to the One on the Right," Newspaper Publishing Independent, January 30, 2005.
4. NCD Risk Factor Collaboration, "A Century of Trends in Adult Human Height," July 26, 2016.
5. Joyce M. Lee and Joel D. Howell, "Tall Girls: The Social Shaping of a Medical Therapy, Arch Pediatric-Adolescent Medicine, 2006.
6. Kae Krysler, "Six-Foot-Three (What Will It Be?)," Los Angeles Times Sunday Magazine, March 28, 1938.

ABOUT THE AUTHOR

Nancy Stancill is the author of two mystery novels, *Saving Texas* and *Winning Texas*, and a retired investigative journalist with the *Houston Chronicle* and *Charlotte (NC) Observer*. She's a journalism graduate of the University of North Carolina and holds a Master of Fine Arts degree from the University of Tampa. She lives in Charlotte with her husband.

NOTE FROM THE AUTHOR

Word-of-mouth is crucial for any author to succeed. If you enjoyed *Tall*, please leave a review online—anywhere you are able. Even if it's just a sentence or two. It would make all the difference and would be very much appreciated.

Thanks!
Nancy

Thank you so much for reading one of Nancy Stancill's books.

If you enjoyed our book, please check out our recommendation for your next great read!

Saving Texas by Nancy Stancill

"A terrific brew of romp, murder, and intrigue."

–Tony D'Souza, author of *Mule*

View other Black Rose Writing titles at www.blackrosewriting.com/books and use promo code **PRINT** to receive a **20% discount** when purchasing.

CPSIA information can be obtained
at www.ICGtesting.com
Printed in the USA
FSHW022325180920
73906FS